Haiku of Love and War:

OIF Perspectives From a Woman's Heart

Haiku of Love and War:

OIF Perspectives From a Woman's Heart

Elyse Braxton

REFLECTION OF GRACE PUBLISHING

copyright © 2017 by Elyse Braxton

All rights reserved. No part of this publication may be reproduced, distributed or transmitted in any form or by any means, including photocopying, recording, or other electronic or mechanical methods, without the prior written permission of the publisher, except in the case of brief quotations embodied in critical reviews and certain other noncommercial uses permitted by copyright law.

Library of Congress Control Number: 2017963417

Reflection Of Grace Publishing

Houston TX/77054

www.reflectionofgrace.net

Book Design : Cover Design / Reflection Of Grace Publishing

Cover Image / lily-studio: James-steidl

Photography/Marisol Williford

ISBN 978-0-9992182-2-8

Dedication

This book is dedicated to the wounded warriors and veterans I have met and served. Thank you.

My love for the troops

Constantly motivates me

Perspective is kept

This book is also dedicated to the women and men of the United States Armed Forces for their selfless service. Seeing you in action makes my heart swell with pride; it is an honor to be your Sailor sister and wear the "cloth of the Nation" along side you. May God bless you and your loved ones for their encouragement and support of the troops.

Lastly, I cannot forget those who made the ultimate sacrifice in the call of duty. You are not forgotten.

If I died in war

Please celebrate my service

To those I'd die for

Acknowledgements

I would like to first and foremost acknowledge God and His Son Jesus Christ, our Lord and Savior, for Their unconditional love, guidance, direction, inspiration, forgiveness, and favor. With Them I am everything, without Them I am nothing.

Thank you to my parents Virginia and Stanley, my brothers Stanley and Evan, relatives, and friends for their support and understanding, especially when Uncle Sam or I made the decision to be apart from them.

A special note of thanks goes out to the Detachment Echo Wave 2 Female Junior Officers I shared living spaces with at Camp Pendleton and Camp Arifjan for their validation and support of my writing of our mutual experiences.

I would have been lost without my Expeditionary Medical Facility Kuwait "family" and military branch-wide "family", during my deployment, as they were often the inspirations for my writings.

Ever in my heart

Nothing like a Mother's love

Mom, you are my world

Introduction

Imagine being placed in a life changing situation where you feel you've lost all control and/or your freedom. There is no end in sight or there is an end that must be endured until completion. What do you do to cope with anxiety and possible fear? How do you handle the monotony and boredom? What if this is something as simple as waiting in line for several hours to ride an amusement park ride or finally board an airplane delayed for maintenance problems? Whether the event is horrific or inconvenient, the power of the mind and one's attitude can make all the difference in the world. Either you surrender to the situation or survive by controlling what you can, no matter how small.

Having hope, humor, belief in their comrades, and faith in God was often the difference between life and death for survivors of concentration camps, Prisoner of War compounds, and hostage detainment facilities. Countless stories have documented the power and creativity of survivors' minds to cope when their bodies were suffering from disease, malnutrition, physical and psychological abuse, and pain. There is no truer statement than "Attitude is everything."

Prelude

I love Sinatra
"The Last Dance" was our first song
It's playing right now

Strong and mighty knight
Your armor shining brightly
Whilst thou dost save me?

I feel so special
Who do I give credit to?
Is this really real?

Ring, ring, ring the phone
I look forward to your call
Ever makes me smile

Words cannot describe
Oh to be loved just for me
I thank God for you

Come into my heart
Take off your shoes and relax
Make yourself at home

Spoiled I am, most true
No one will compare to you
Oh those poor suitors

A beautiful nurse
Her heroic fireman
Lovers and servants

To give and receive
We are partners and a team
Serving each other

In the house of God
Holding hands as we worship
Pure Heaven on Earth

Satisfied, complete
If I would die tomorrow
You showed me true love

Love at its apex
This is just the beginning
With no end in sight

Deliciously safe
In your arms forever more
Two souls connecting

Chase me all you want
I will dodge and evade you
Until you are caught

Whoever thought love
Could inspire poetry?
Never thought I would

Our relationship
The ebb and flow of the tide
Finding its way home

Rich indeed I am
My heart won the lottery
Claim ticket in hand

I sleep well at night
During my waking hours
It's all about you

What a risk it is
To share my inner self with you
Yet I feel so free!

I really miss you
You're in control this minute
I gave it to you

The joy of marriage
Partner, lover, teammate, friend
One day at a time

How do we show love?
It's really rather simple
"Just show up", we say

Mutual support
Our goals, dreams, and desires
All in God's timing

I do not exist
It is not ME anymore
Me is now a WE

Planning our wedding
Can't wait for the honeymoon
First the reception

Haiku of Love and War

Elyse Braxton

A long distance love
Unbelievable to most
True and amazing

I feel beautiful
Because the way you love me
Makeup optional

Heads bowed, hands held tight
Praying for one another
True intimacy

To say, "I love you"
A perfect understatement
How I really feel

Chosen just for me
Your gifts of wine and roses
Intoxicating

You have got the key
I trust you with all my heart
My partner, my love

Pure and natural
So effortless is our love
You are worth the wait

A relationship
Founded on solid friendship
Grounded in the Lord

A most precious gift
You have given me your heart
As I have to you

Not doing a thing
We could watch paint dry together
Because it is YOU!

Vulnerable girl
Come into my little world
You will protect me

Your love is so strong
You make my life worth living
Let's make memories

Predeployment

That Monday morning
"You're deploying to Kuwait"
Life never the same

Fear of the unknown
What is deployment about?
I am not prepared

My tears start to well
A strong shoulder you provide
I feel better now

First time deployee
Honored to serve, but I'm scared
I really need help

The tearful goodbye
As we part at the airport
It hurts to leave you

The longest goodbye
As I'm off to go to war
My man stays behind

Sneaking a last kiss
My destiny awaits me
Road to deployment

Leaving for Kuwait
Crying in the terminal
Such uncertainty

Two scared young nurses
Saying goodbye to loved ones
Overcome by tears

Who will watch the kids?
Kiss and tuck them in at night?
How does a Mom feel?

Does she feel guilty?
Uncle Sam versus the kids
Sam gets her this time

Will I get the call?
What if something bad happens?
A Red Cross Message

Our in-processing
Lots and lots of paperwork
Soon the show will start

Camp Pendleton

Lying on my cot
Calm before the desert storm
Thoughts of you all day

Hurry up and wait!
My deployment to Kuwait
Semper Gumby, yeah!

Ten-hut, SEA hut 10
Sleeping with 13 sisters
Eating MRE's

No real traffic jams
Eight toilets and group showers
And 80 women

What? My shorts are wet!
Sitting on my Camelbak®
Hate when that happens

We have a curfew
Back on base by 9 pm
Public shame if late

Plenty of down time
We must savor the freedom
As we're not "locked in"

Support from my love
I am forever grateful
War brings us closer

Haiku of Love and War

Church at Pendleton
I let my guard down, tears flow
In my Father's house

Email and texting
So close yet so far away
Communication

Heads bowed, hands held tight
Praying for one another
True intimacy

I am determined
Trying to get cell access
To say, "I love you"

More plumbing problems
Septic system overload
Porta-potty time!

At pistol practice
I want to hit the target
Earn a new medal

It really is fun
Shooting paper not people
NEVER at people

I was successful
Second try - I'm a marksman
Sense of achievement

Knowing you love me
Will sustain me in wartime
Can't wait to see you!

The sound of your voice
Soothing, calming, loving me
Music to my ears

I'm feeling guilty
The enlisted work so hard
Officers, show up

How do they do it?
Working in all that MOPP gear
For hours on end

Adventures abound
Convoy and litter training
Not reality

Funny what you'll do
When you're serving your country
This is just training

Off base liberty
I'm grateful to stand the watch
Give back to my team

Last chance for freedom
Overnight in a hotel
With a double bed!

My fidelity
Entwined rings around your neck
Bring them back to me

Haiku of Love and War

I wear your dog tag
Loving reminder of faith
Tangible keepsake

You are a love song
Waiting for a melody
That I want to sing

To be missing you
Hearts, bodies disconnected
A break in the link

Sitting on my cot
Tears of fear overcome me
I get a group hug

Our gear loaded up
We are all assigned a bus
Up to the air base

Some tearful goodbyes
To my family on the phone
I'll see them next year

Laughing and bonding
Playing cards with enlisted
Lifetime memories

Leaving for Kuwait
Crying in the terminal
Fear of the unknown

We're lined up by rank
Preparing to board the plane
Please, a window seat

Landing in Bangor
Welcomed by the Maine Greeters
Last time in the States

Camp Arifjan

The plane is landing
Mariner's cross in my hand
Welcome to Kuwait

Reality hits
We are in a combat zone
Security high

I say the Lord's Prayer
As there's no turning back now
My country's at war

It's all fun and games
Protected in the airplane
Soon we have to land

Wartime medicine
Lifetime opportunity
Some will never know

One hundred forty
What the thermometer read
While we unload trucks

Base water main broke
Baby wipe shower tonight
Glamorous is war

Claustrophobia
Olive drab swaddling cloth
Army sleeping bag

What's that sound I hear?
Loud voices outside our tent
Protect me, Father

Is it Arabic?
Voices getting louder
In God I shall trust

Footsteps crunch gravel
Sleeping in a combat zone
Are we really safe?

Having faith not fear
Now I lay me down to sleep
I must be street smart

Be very careful
Always on the alert now
Don't let your guard down

Now the power's out
Taking showers by flashlight
Slightly romantic

My battle buddy
I can't leave home without one
No more solitude

Oh to have 'me' time
No one to lead or follow
Need a hiding place

Life behind curtains
And concertina wire
It's for our safety

Over the PA
Weekly Kuwaiti bombings
They are planned events

The DSN line
How I long to hear your voice
The hot line to love

Despite the stressors
I hear the smile in your voice
Whenever we talk

Is it possible?
Someone to call my soulmate?
Apparently so

My sensitive man
Your tears are not shed in vain
I kiss them away

Sinatra was right
Yes, I concentrate on you
My sweet happy place

Haiku of Love and War

Several women
Don't have a tent-ture tantrum
In a little space

Could be a lot worse
Body armor, guns, AND heat
Keep the perspective

Not really homesick
I miss garlic and soy milk
But not together

Fruity shower gel
Spa time in war time
A simple pleasure

Oooo, it's the mail call!
Happy to get your letter
Beaming the whole day

The hardest part is
Not seeing you with good news
Smiling back at me

My inspiration
You are my everything
Love without borders

Sleep, eat, and workout
Every day is Monday
My workday routine

Sleeping for night shift
My considerate tent mates
What angels they are

Staying up real late
So my body stays on nights
Not an easy feat

I watched two movies
To pass the time while I'm up
I might see a third

I LOVE your support
And the fact you are so proud
I can't stop smiling

I the Boot Ensign
A most revered position
One and only one

Dubious honor
Lowest ranking Officer
In all of Kuwait

It's filled with concrete
My 14-pound combat boot
Also a weapon

No chances of theft
The Ensign boot is hidden
Under my pillow

Boot for companion
We run errands together
Never leaves my side

Elyse Braxton — Haiku of Love and War

My boot is my friend
A great conversation piece
Symbol of stature

Told I'm a "legend"
I got the CNO to sign
The Ensign Boot

It's too late to call
Desiring to hear you live
Thank God for voice mail

We are not at war
It's a beach vacation
With long sleeves and pants

In music and food
Thoughts of you everywhere
Always on my mind

Miles apart we are
So close yet so far away
Two hearts become one

A painful lecture
Series of redundancy
Somebody shoot me

We share a bunk bed
Rank has its privileges
Someday, my own room

My mind keeps racing
It is hard to go to sleep
Come, Mr. Sandman

Despite the distance
We still share the galaxy
Twinkling in the sky

The sound of your voice
Soothing, calming, loving me
Music to my ears

We may move forward
Rifle training tomorrow
Serving my country

Will you volunteer?
I am scared to go to war
God will go with me

I welcome the chance
To provide nursing up north
Change of scenery

Kuwait City

Got an off-base pass
Trip into Kuwait City
We got out of "jail"

Dressed in black garments
Woman's wear in the Grand Mosque
Many photo ops

Elyse Braxton — Haiku of Love and War

Touring the inside
Looking like Islamic Nuns
We females explored

Overpriced buffet
Within the Kuwait Towers
The event: priceless

Dad's been to Towers
He had run of the city
I'm grateful for eggs

Watching the people
In Arab and western wear
NOT in camouflage

Along the highway
Bedouins set up their tents
Where are the camels?

Despite the freedom
We had to have armed escorts
Everywhere we drove

In the Al Khout Mall
Cinnabon wafts in the air
We HAVE to partake

Must be respectful
Do not talk to the locals
And NO photographs

So slow on Sunday
We forgot it's a work day
Friday's their Sabbath

Groundhog Day

Walking the compound
I like to spread some sunshine
Ev'rywhere I go

Missing puzzle piece
Laying in the desert sand
Lost and all alone

So life is a beach
Is this Jersey or Kuwait?
Where is the boardwalk?

Patients in the ward
Appreciation they give
Job satisfaction

My head on your chest
Your shirt is my pillowcase
I sleep peacefully

Every love song
Was written for you and me
Maybe we should share

The Kuwaiti moon
Shining in the desert sky
Warm at 3 am

A clean uniform
Dancing in my combat boots
Salsa anyone?

Elyse Braxton   Haiku of Love and War

Getting settled in
The permanence of working
Our battle rhythm

Friendship and respect
Ours is a mutual love
Growing like a weed

I'm a risk taker
You say you love my boldness
I feel safe with you

Like a Storm Trooper
Body armor and Kevlar
My "battle rattle"

Oh my precious sleep
Not enough, taken quickly
But, it could be worse

Supplemental help
Independent Augmentee
An honor to serve

Navy Core Values
Honor, Courage, Commitment
Handbook for living

In spite of distance
We seem closer than ever
I hear, "You've got mail!"

I save your letters
In the pillow on my bed
Loving me to sleep

My strong mighty knight
I want to be there for you
When you are in need

Whether near or far
A powerful thing, our love
Sustenance

Sweet wonderful you
Greater than my wildest dreams
God really knows best

Oh the reunion
Hold you in my arms and kiss
Gaze into your eyes

It's jam packed with love
How can you get so much care?
In that little box?

How do I love thee?
Letters with a lipstick kiss
A small reminder

We let our guard down
Our vulnerabilities
Deeper our love grows

I used to believe
Diamonds are a girl's best friend
Until I met you

Elyse Braxton — Haiku of Love and War

Is this a lyric?
"You're all I've ever wanted"
Maybe it should be

Life is much better
As we take it side by stride
Enjoying the view

Here where you belong
You can call my heart your home
I'll leave the light on

When I'm on the phone
I imagine I'm with you
My head on your chest

Online, on the phone
We communicate daily
Never really left

I count the minutes
Till I can call you again
An eternity

Your voice is so clear
But we can't reach out and touch
Need a TOUCH tone phone

I was so homesick
Hearing our country music
Almost left the place

Anticipation
When will I see you again?
Practice in patience

On the patio
Hanging with the Latinos
My new happy place

Hugging my patient
Supportive ear, hand to hold
Nursing equals love

As the clock ticks down
I become more ecstatic
Because I can call

The joy of your voice
When I'm silent on the phone
I am just beaming

The smiling Ensign
Taking around the big brass
Just like family

The gift of garlic
Bringing me a taste from home
How thoughtful you are

I couldn't hug you
Perception and protocol
There'll be a raincheck

The junior Ensign
Senior Officers lined up
She does what she wants

Haiku of Love and War

Elyse Braxton

We exchange greetings
The butter bar and 4-star
I'm running the show

For just a second
A familiar face from home
Removes loneliness

Cradled in my arms
The 14-pound combat boot
Navy tradition

It is hard to sleep
You inspire poetry
As I relive love

Thrill ride of our life
Hitching your dreams to my star
As I do to you

The White House or not
I will be your First Lady
Supporting her man

I am the diamond
Your prongs give me the best light
We are beautiful

Constant amazement
Multifaceted you are
You captivate me

I love how we talk
Getting to know each other
No subject too deep

When I'm not speaking
I am interrupting you
Heart mile a minute

Our secret language
Innuendos and word play
They won't understand

My mind gathers speed
As we scholarly engage
Matching wit for wit

Of all the women
You've come across in your life
You have chosen me

I should be sleeping
Can't stop thinking about you
An infinite love

Try, try as we must
Patience is not a virtue
That comes easily

When we're insecure
We believe in each other
The backbone of love

We share our support
And validate each other
Isn't that divine?

Oatmeal and mixed nuts
The breakfast of champions
Sometimes a donut

Walking in the sand
Combat boots are glass slippers
Come my stately prince

The joy of your voice
When I'm silent on the phone
I am just beaming

Deployment is hard
For those whose love is like sand
Ours is like marble

Rare and precious gift
We will live the love story
Yet to be written

My eyes grow heavy
Yet I want to talk with you
So I type away

Bright eyes, blushing cheeks
You are better than makeup
I am radiant

How do I show love
In 17 syllables?
It's not hard at all

We are in accord
With almost everything
'Cause I'm always right

Now that I know you
I can spot a counterfeit
You are the real deal

Words cannot describe
The depth of my love for you
In just one poem

Emotions so raw
Describing the devotion
And strength of our love

Our eyes are closed tight
We paint pictures on the phone
Internalizing

Thanks for being there
You are easy to run to
For comfort and love

My former patient
Asked me to his birthday lunch
He brought me some cake

Who am I to judge?
War brings out the worst in folks
I throw love not stones

Always standing out
A goldfish with a big smile
In the desert pond

Elyse Braxton — Haiku of Love and War

My mariner's cross
Perfect in every way
Never taken off

Familiar faces
As we go about our day
Making this a home

Kindness from strangers
I dole out my gratitude
They didn't have to

What was the moment?
That defined my love for you
I can't recollect

Smittenization
What happens when men meet me
A gift or a curse?

In this deployment
Less alienated here
Compared to my home

It's still a man's world
Some men don't want women here
Let's just get along

Your love is a drug
I can't get enough of you
You're an addiction

There will be hard days
Missing at an all-time high
Yet we will connect

Sunday and Monday
Loneliest days of the week
In a little funk

I'm glad you feel free
To let the real you come forth
With grand acceptance

It is an honor
To be your support network
As you venture out

I say, "Go for it!"
I will be your greatest fan
Your success is mine

I find when I'm blue
Poetry keeps perspective
And my heart working

Can't forget our God
Let's get back to the Bible
To keep us grounded

Poetry writing
Much better than therapy
Heart medication

Chatting on the phone
Re-loving the memories
Such a day maker

Elyse Braxton — Haiku of Love and War

Saying "I love you"
In several languages
Means so much to me

Some people pick fights
When they want some attention
A cry out for love

Our love grew and grows
You took me off the market
Just by appearing

Through good times and bad
Our unconditional love
Will weather the storm

I must keep the faith
There are times of impatience
God is not done yet

Remember the day?
We went from friends to lovers
No, I can't either

Not a crescendo
Just an ongoing building
Of my love for you

We don't know the dates
As they are not important
In the scheme of things

After all these months
Do you still get butterflies
Whenever we meet?

Monday is lonely
Tonight I will swim and dance
Then I'll be better

Bailando salsa (dancing salsa)
Mis amigos Latinos (my latin friends)
Casa nueva (new home)

Pain in my stomach
Visceral anxiety
Hollow and empty

My shorts are too short
No, skinny legs are too long
Stupid Army rules

Two months and a day
Since we headed off to war
Loved ones left behind

The smallest trigger
Familiar foods and music
Make me think of you

Your face crystal clear
The curves and texture from touch
Always on my mind

I long to touch you
Hold you in my arms and kiss
I've said this before

The sign on my heart
Reads in bold letters: **Taken**
Truth be told: Given

The stroke of a pen
Your letters of assurance
Unbeknownst to you

The power of sight
Mirrors to our very soul
As we gaze deeply

We have concluded
No word can describe our love
In any language

Accelerated
We have taken a lifetime
Of love really slow

Sharing the scriptures
Long distance Bible study
Again brings us close

It's the little things
You found a way to my heart
That bring big rewards

When I hear your voice
Bye bye insecurity
The world is all right

Just the name Iraq
Makes me shiver to my bones
The land of hatred

Not a true break up
A romantic downsizing
Return to friendship

The pain and the tears
Repairing what was broken
Friend-ly superglue

New rules to follow
Agreeing to set limits
Joint forces remain

Our friendship so strong
Despite the hardship
The closer we grow

Watching what we say
No rekindling of passion
We will not defraud

The highest respect
Mutual admiration
Reciprocal pride

My heart is off hold
Yet I am still receptive
If timing is right

The power's off here
In our open bay barracks
An eerie silence

Haiku of Love and War

Elyse Braxton

For my well being
No sentimentality
I don't like to cry

No generator
Our hearing finely attuned
Constant white noise gone

Day of rest Sunday
Time to recharge and prepare
Hard when you're alone

Special morale call
Lifting you from Sunday blues
You're happy, me too

It is not easy
Giving tough love to a friend
Yet this is true love

You already know
When it comes to love and war
I do not fight fair

Same team, new dance steps
Our laughter is palpable
As we try new words

With no end in sight
I was growing impatient
Our timing was off

Inconsequential
Talking with you for hours
Time stands still for us

Love of thesaurus
Helps me find the perfect word
When I'm at a loss

I'll be there for you
Every step of the way
Here, at war, and back

You are all around
Yet I can't dwell on the past
It is how I cope

The power is back!
Our noises to our self now
Drowned by the humming

Only just begun
Keeping it in perspective
We are half way there

Gave your gifts away
Cardio-protective move
Reduced my heartache

Now THIS is the time
We lay down at the altar
Sacrifice for God

We're ever mindful
Beautiful humility
Of how we've been blessed

Music to God's ears
Constant words of love and praise
Coming from our heart

Jesus bore it all
Dying on the cross for us
To atone our sins

Haiku therapy
Better than psychologists
Takes the stress away

The initial pain
Starts our communication
The healing begins

Growing pains are real
As they say, "No pain, no gain"
Another growth-spurt

Some would say it's odd
That which would weaken others
Only strengthens us

New rules and boundaries
Redefined relationship
Learning as we GrOw

Such a strong friendship
Shared laughter from memories
An unbroken bond

Forged in a foundry
Tempered like fine stainless steel
Friendship tough as nails

The love of Jesus
Tattooed boldly on our heart
For the world to see

Your gift of friendship
I'll never take for granted
I KNOW God's blessings

When I used to say
It's the God in me you see
You now understand

Channeling feelings
A simple redirection
To destination

A relationship
Is what Jesus truly wants
From those He loves

My heart ached so much
Oh how I cried that Thursday
I was in such pain

When it comes to love
I have learned over the years
Not to hold my breath

Your encouragement
Keeps me writing and writing
Often just for you

Emulating Christ
We use our power for good
As we spread the love

You are my best friend
Hand delivered by our God
Because He loves me

He's an on-time God
If we have patience and wait
It's hard but worth it

Safe in your presence
Engaging conversation
Your love of my faults

All-time favorite?
You opening my car door
I eat that stuff up!

Hours on the phone
It's just like the good old days
We're insatiable

My silence is odd
I listen more than you think
To use against you

You spark my mind so
I interrupt like a flame
My brain is tinder

My freedom to cry
The music and fellowship
Worshipping in church

We all have God's gifts
Special talents and knowledge
He gave me you, too

Monday blues are gone
I will treasure my day off
I am so thankful

Funny, without sight
You can see my reactions
When we're on the phone

Nothing is missing
Full array of emotions
In your heart's tool box

You sit by the phone
Our loving expectancy
Can't wait to leave work

Morning wake-up call
Preparing to start our day
Aren't time zones the best?

Two super powers
Using our forces for good
We're synergistic

You've offered yourself
My point guard and run-to man
I give in return

Haiku of Love and War

Elyse Braxton

No more future talk
Living the present and past
Ensures a future

Nothing against you
My lowered expectations
Ensure endurance

Music to my heart
I like to know I'm needed
Mostly by you, though

Out in the open
You have an outlet in me
Sharing your feelings

Giggling on the phone
Memories last a laugh-time
A wonderful life

Changing our focus
Thoughts and desires remain
Just new behavior

Jesus at the helm
He guides me to still water
Anchored to safety

Everything seems right
As if we were custom made
Just for each other

I've known a few frogs
Maybe someone else's prince
You are my true KING

You are my David
You outsmart the enemy
With knowledge as stones

Talk about the love
Two boxes AND a letter
My long distance hugs

Running like the wind
A treadmill athlete is born
Man does my butt hurt

In a crowded room
Feels like we're the only two
World nonexistent

When I close my eyes
You appear just like magic
Oh so vividly

The gift of suspense
I enjoy surprising you
Presents from my heart

It is an honor
That you cry in front of me
Symbol of true strength

I am truly touched
By your depth of emotion
Thus I start to share

Haiku of Love and War

All the things we do
Summarized very simply
That word would be: Love

I am serious
We are every love song
Past, present, future

I am less fearful
As I place this in God's hands
He has full control

PA announcement
Uniforms in the DFAC
A heightened alert

Wouldn't it be nice?
Kiss under the mistletoe
In Southwest Asia

Sand gets in my ears
As the wind dances around
Where is the music?

Reading both our minds
Finishing our sentences
Isn't it scary?

Thirty extra pounds
Only for a few hours
Our body armor

I am so thankful
Despite the bad press of war
Nurses get support

Tea cup and a spoon
Talk about divine timing
A gift from Colleen

Despite the laughter
We still make time for Jesus
Our Lord and Savior

A mind full of peace
Heart devoted to service
All part of God's will

Gone for a whole year
A true possibility
Fraction of my life

So far, adjusting
Occasional blue moments
Short in duration

A special day off
Lots of nurses, few patients
Now I can two-step

Five hours of light
In our open bay barracks
Got to maximize

He might have cancer
I saw a change in his mood
He is not married

Haiku of Love and War

A kiss on the hand
As we mutually charm
What a sweet patient

I wish you were here
Sitting side by side at church
You were in my mind

Our eyes fail to see
The story of Gideon
God doesn't make junk

A gift from my heart
A haiku written for you
As you mean so much

In my happy place
Whether salsa or two-step
I am just beaming

An audible smile
When I'm listening to you
And am not talking

A few are smitten
Because of my happy vibes
You bring out my best

Cooler are the days
As I relatively speak
Still in the eighties

When you say a prayer
You have GOT to move your feet
There is no FedEx

How will we handle
The first time we reunite?
We'll use oven mitts

I like the ER
It's Family Practice on crack
Great observation

What a reunion
I can't wait till we're stateside
We'll be sequestered

Wow, two months Monday
One third down, two thirds to go
Where has the time gone?

Sensitivity
Sets you apart from the rest
You are a true gift

Secure in your love
It's actually freeing
I know where home is

Misplaced your letter
I'm searching throughout my room
Relief, it was found

Please, what did I do
To have won a man like you?
Gotta tell the girls

Haiku of Love and War

Elyse Braxton

What's on your wish list?
I hope we have a lifetime
To see, do, and be

I can't believe it
I am so in love with you
You're my everything

Like a hand in glove
Our compatibility
A most perfect fit

Repeating our words
The glue that keeps our bond tight
How you make me feel

You're so beautiful
Can't take my eyes off of you
And those gorgeous legs

It's a guarantee
Amazing Grace makes me cry
Recalling His love

Never been stronger
Our great communication
And relationship

Sometimes I get sad
Reflecting on rejection
From boys in the past

How can they see it?
Hidden in a uniform
I'm Ugly Betty!

Our high school photos
Will ever keep us humble
When egos get too big

When we say goodnight
All the way home I'll be warm
Not just at Christmas

Adult and mature
We chose each other
Till death do us part

Where does the time go?
An hour seems like minutes
Chatting on the phone

We are committed
Daily communication
Steroids for our love

You say I'm gorgeous
And that every man can see
Still don't believe you

Happening already
Someone wants to marry me
Says my friend Ruben

The Sergeant Major
Knows not the competition
My heart is taken

Haiku of Love and War

Clothes fitting better
Feeling of accomplishment
I like working out

My muscles feel sore
I like the feeling of strength
No pain thus no gain

Oh so natural
We're truly compatible
Our flaws are deemed cute

Grandmother would say
Beauty is as beauty does
You're SO beautiful

My value goes up
The more they come after me
Because I'm all yours

I'll wait patiently
For however long it takes
All I want is you

It's incurable
Deeply profound love for you
Greatest affliction

I'm truly flattered
Others find me appealing
As Ugly Betty

I live for Wednesday
For it is surf and turf night
Crab leg memories

I'm stuffed to the gills
If your love had calories
I'd be overweight

When I look at you
I see nothing but pure love
And thank God again

Live or in photos
I love to look in your eyes
A soul connection

Constant state of awe
Gazing in your eyes while dancing
State of unbelief

I am the Swiss Miss
Neutral when it comes to men
You're an exception

Daily devotions
Giving credit where it's due
Shared over the phone

Our love is like God
Indescribable beauty
Beyond wildest dreams

Others are boring
Compared to your character
I just appease them

Haiku of Love and War

Incomparable
You're the man for all seasons
Reasons, my lifetime

Is it my brownness?
The locals come out in droves
When I exercise

You, me, Christmas tree
The birth of baby Jesus
He's the real reason

The Navy's Birthday
First desert 5K
One step at a time

Lift first, then the heart
For fat loss and muscle gain
I'll give it a try

More than one have said
When I'm on the running path
I have a good pace

On the Corpsmen's list
I'm a certified hottie
Talk about flattered

My heart beats faster
When you state your persistence
For winning my heart

Intimidating
Being watched when I workout
What are they thinking?

I'm missing your touch
I long to be in your arms
Head on your shoulder

I've let my guard down
Crying jags like none other
You are there for me

I love you so much
Too large to enumerate
Or put into words

Talk about creepy
I saw the Sandman today
Man doesn't give up!

I can smell the prowl
As the Sandman approaches
Dude, just go away!

I like the soreness
A day after working out
The challenge is pleasing

You're so amazing
I'm turning into a snob
Other men bore me

Almost time for church
Good word, music, and people
I wish you were here

Elyse Braxton   Haiku of Love and War

As I've said before
Your love is the greatest gift
I've ever received

Through all of my days
The sustenance of your love
Has a hold on me

Even if they tried
Nobody does it better
The way you love me

I'm not really sore
After yesterday's 5k
I'm getting stronger

Slowly and surely
Fitness goals are paying off
See? Feel the results

I like deployments
They see me as an adult
Not just an Ensign

The Commander's Cup
I was hauling tail in sand
Great for an "olde" gal

Latin music plays
Our island life in Kuwait
A breeze is blowing

I grab a partner
For some serious salsa
I can't stop smiling

I'm always smiling
There are so many reasons
You're the biggest part

Talk about humbled
A Corpsman said I was missed
During my day off

Incredibly blessed
If God's favor was water
I'd be soaking wet

We made a mistake
Commander brought us all in
Afterwards, gun shy

Today's the first day
I brought out your old letters
I read of our love

I am SO content
My heart is safely with you
Beating next to yours

To have and to hold
I miss being in your arms
A feeling of home

Mirrors of the soul
I can't get over your eyes
Reflection of love

Elyse Braxton — Haiku of Love and War

We switch to day shift
A new set of challenges
To conquer and win

I don't feel worthy
When folks want to send me stuff
You're an exception

Hope to have muscle
I want to tighten and tone
Lose a little fat

You're the greatest thing
Since sliced whole clove garlic bread
I'm talkin' awesome!

He sits and watches
It's a little unnerving
When I'm jumping rope

Perfectly content
How you always make me feel
By you being you

The Continental
Sinatra sang of this dance
We need to learn this

You are my Shipmate
I put your life before mine
As you do for me

Laughing with Skipper
Not so intimidating
Yet he's still, "The Boss"

Surprise phone attack
Caught you totally off guard
We can't stop smiling

Just like olden times
As we schedule our phone calls
Shunning the distance

Impactful sermon
My shipmate was moved to tears
I gave him a hug

God forgives all sins
Through the blood of Jesus Christ
Free for repenting

DNS Team 3
My hospital family
Genuine caring

A great group of folks
We've relied on each other
As a family

No hurdle too small
Or timeframe unspecified
To work for your love

Although I'm their age
They are Commanders, I'm not
I feel like a kid

Haiku of Love and War

Elyse Braxton

Not a healthy meal
A bag of potato chips
Eaten all at once

Some days you're mushy
Some days you're just hormonal
Love you just the same

I drove a Humvee!
Haven't driven since July
Still know what to do

Hung out in my room
I was really missing you
SO wish I was there

Never thought I knew
I'd miss your emails that much
Till they stopped coming

Here in the ER
Once again, thinking of you
Talking about eyes

The days are cooler
Goodbye to triple digits
Rainy season soon

Moustache October
Some men were quite successful
Little Wardroom fun

Almost like college
Eating meals in PT gear
No dress to impress

Sporting my moustache
I could still eat gracefully
Thank God for napkins

My sexy cat ears
The guys were looking at me
Or it felt that way

Tour the haunted house
A Kuwaiti Halloween
Play carnival games

Our little setback
Provided maximum growth
As our love matures

Love is like money
The interest keeps growing
The more we invest

Think I've got the slump
Can look but don't want to touch
Saving THAT for you

Again, only me
I have to shoot left-handed
Hope I qualify!

Knowledge of God's love
New friends wherever I go
It's the God in me

Elyse Braxton — Haiku of Love and War

Psychotic patient
We're not supposed to touch him
How can I show love?

I am tickled pink!
Qualified on the rifle
Shooting left-handed

Baskin and Robbins
Sliced red, green, yellow peppers
Little tastes of home

Puerto Kuwaito
People playing dominoes
Music in the breeze

My motherly love
Comforting to my patients
I see them as sons

I'm hard on myself
I want to grow and excel
To be Super Nurse

Laughing on the phone
Private jokes only we get
Keeps us ever close

What do I look like?
This time I'm Algerian
Exotic beauty

Twenty years younger
There's this one gorgeous Corpsman
But I'm no cougar

I love life on Earth
Yet Heaven is my true home
Divine mission trip

With me by your side
There's nothing you cannot do
You are my hero

The smile in your voice
Is deafening when we talk
Hard to hear your words

Incomparable
There's no other man like you
My search is over

Talk about heartache
We lost one the other day
Knots in my stomach

Nothing more tragic
Than a young person dying
Hopes and years vanish

Had help from my friends
To support me in the loss
Forever grateful

Compartmentalize
I cannot be paralyzed
By major setbacks

Haiku of Love and War

Determined you are
With defiant directness
To capture my heart

Oh how I love you
Emotional connection
Not to be undone

We are halfway done
Time flies when it's Groundhog Day
I'll miss my shipmates

Crab legs on Wednesday
No matter who I am with
I'm thinking of you

Aren't I special?
Standing invites to MARCENT
I love my Marines!

When I'm at MARCENT
The announcement is "Red Badge"
Upon my entry

I finished the run
Glamorously tossing cookies
In the track's trash can

Ever a standout
Me, the red and green "Marine"
With skinny brown legs

I'm going to stay
For a year-long deployment
Three quarters to go

My morale is down
Skipper leads on the sidelines
Not in the trenches

Where is the respect?
One cannot micromanage
And praise together

Human frailties
I will shield you all I can
With reassurance

The smell of sawdust
You are pleasantly surprised
That we share this too

Retail therapy
I will never understand
God is my spackle

Some things don't seem fair
Must look at the big picture
God means it for good

A smile on my face
Latin rhythm in my heart
Feet are happy too

Providing comfort
To a young mourning soldier
After his friend's death

Haiku of Love and War

Elyse Braxton

I do not feel pure
When I touch my black patients
They are dark and rich

Don't get me wrong though
I'm perfectly shade matched too
By God, the Father

Talking skin color
"As light as Ensign Braxton?"
Said the Senior Chief

I wouldn't have known
If not for decorations
It's Thanksgiving Day

I love to see flash
When the needle hits a vein
Feeling of success

Perfectly in love
In emotional Eden
A true gift from God

Too many moments
To count my validation
Of why you're God's best

Out of the woodwork
The suitors are out for me
Sorry guys, taken

Love at its finest
We have perfected the moves
A dance of courtship

You are family
As far as I am concerned
Now and forever

Cannot imagine
Spending my life without you
That would be torture

With my two weeks off
I will visit Australia
Free from Uncle Sam

Our values differ
We are not equally yoked
But I'll be his friend

My heart is stubborn
I'm with folks, mind and body
Yet it won't leave you

I know I'm strong willed
God tested that years ago
I'm grateful I lost

Must stay positive
And watch what I want to say
It won't serve me well

Must pray for Skipper
Dismiss negativity
He is God's child too

Do you really know
Just how beautiful you are
To me and my soul?

It has been two months
Since we downsized our romance
Our love is stronger

My heart is heavy
My impatience is growing
Exponentially

I was in your dream
I jumped down into your arms
Now, reality

We can overcome
There'll be more good times than bad
We will celebrate

I was mad at you
I couldn't get through to you
It was your ringer

I found my wallet
A major sigh of relief
Your card was in it

So what if I have moods?
Please don't discount my hormones
Every girl has them

Yes, he is a friend
But he's not a dinner guest
You're beyond compare

I feel so callous
Not emotionally attached
As he seems to be

Maybe it's the stress
That heightens my emotions
I am embarrassed

He's selling himself
When he asked what I look for
I am not shopping

He said it himself
I am too tall for most men
But he'll dance with me

Inquisitive men
See my childlike innocence
Read me like a book

I saw the Sandman
Came up and gave me a hug
Thankfully he left

Oh I love Jesus
If I were the only one
He still would have died

I'm getting older
Don't know these modern-day songs
Rather proud of it

Haiku of Love and War

Keeping his secret
Skipper was a cheerleader
My eyes just sparkle

I love the woodshop
I get lost in the sawdust
I don't want to leave

The sanding machines
Instant gratification
So soft to the touch

Many ideas
For potential wood projects
This is exciting

Longer deployment
A larger family to love
Lifetime memories

Joy of woodworking
Never thought I was crafty
In a girly way

Wood is practical
The projects will be useful
Not dust collectors

A lazy day off
My laundry's in the dryer
I'm chilling in bed

I am feeling fat
I really need to work out
Get my body back

Yes, Navy's got jokes
Laughter will heal everything
A contagious smile

I've learned not to judge
Considering my patients
And their frailties

Only two months more
Say goodbye to Ensign-hood
I will miss that rank

You asked for one trait
What I love best about you
It's "respect", hands down

Respect umbrella
Covers chivalry and trust
As well as safety

I lose track of time
Working in the woodshop
Absorbed by my crafts

Special liberty
Deserved after yesterday
On to the woodshop!

I saw the photo
Of the girl who died on base
In the Navy Times

Elyse Braxton — Haiku of Love and War

You've made yourself clear
I am yours and yours alone
Show me the diamond!

My little campus
Greeted by former patients
Jail life is cozy

Working overseas
I like the intimacy
We're all together

In a big command
There's no one to come home to
Here, I'm surrounded

New work assignment
I am scared to leave the floor
But it's for my growth

Where will I go next?
Maybe Asia or Europe
God leads, I follow

Europe would be cool
I would like to run around
When I have free time

In for the long run
Will you really follow me
Till I retire?

Now, it's about me
Until I am really caught
Thanks for the freedom

Frank sings our heart's songs
Yet it's hard to choose which one
We'll take all of them

I can work the crowd
Although I am Lady Luck
I come home to you

Manic Depressive
A high energy level
His meds wouldn't work

Reading patient's charts
They've really been through a lot
This keeps me humble

Another payday
And soon I'll get a big raise
Pay my loans faster

That familiar cough
Because of years of smoking
Our Divo is back

The ward is quiet
All the psych patients are gone
Off to Germany

Hanging out in sweats
I feel like I'm in college
But now I get paid

Elyse Braxton — Haiku of Love and War

Sexy cheerleader
Navy shorts, cover and boots
Like how my hips move?

Seducing the crowd
You're who I'm performing for
In my subtle ways

Needs not being met
My eyes are starting to stray
But I will not act

This is a cruel joke
I am loved but not wanted
In the normal way

Doubts are creeping in
Hey, call me when you're ready
I don't like to share

Scared to take a dip
Into the pool of dating
I don't swim that well

Is there one for me?
A helpmate I belong to?
A strong man of faith?

Don't know what to do
I think I'll marry my job
It's a guarantee

I already know
There are more Christian women
Not all get a man

Desire pursuit
By someone who wants me now
I'm feeling lonely

Aren't I the fool?
Waiting indefinitely
For what I don't know

Every girl has dreams
For unconditional love
To give and receive

His mission cut short
Wife kept calling the command
Now they're divorcing

Jesus, take me home
I am really suffering
You are my true love

There's not much to say
Not giving the joy you need
Wasting your minutes

Nothing you can do
You want to remove my pain
Really, there's nothing

Making eye contact
Exchanging small pleasantries
Would like to know you

Elyse Braxton — Haiku of Love and War

Do you look at me
The same way I look at you?
Or am I dreaming?

The strong silent type
As he goes for more coffee
Command's single dad

I'm always happy
Whenever you cross my path
We are both so shy

You played really well
I would scan the field for you
Did you look for me?

Did you see me dance?
I was in my happy place
Do you have rhythm?

What is your story?
We've only chatted briefly
I'd hang out with you

A chance encounter
You saw me get my hair done
You sat next to me

Soon I'll work night shift
May see you in the morning
Maybe not at all

I hope I can help
Depending where you're stationed
Someone to hang with

It's good to have friends
To give and receive support
In our times of need

I dream of romance
To share an intimate bond
Love like none other

Best friend desired
To share the good times and bad
And hot fudge sundaes

There's trust in women
They only want my friendship
No stringing along

Don't feel like calling
There's really not much to say
But I will oblige

How will your hand feel?
Will we get sparks at first touch?
That is important

Not a true science
But chemistry's important
For relationships

To have chemistry
Need an emotional bond
That's just for starters

Elyse Braxton — Haiku of Love and War

I had a great love
But it wasn't meant to be
I got impatient

I have high standards
Not many men reach that mark
I will not settle

Tis better single
Than alone yet together
That is more painful

Will I meet someone
To completely satisfy
Or am I dreaming?

Safe haven in church
To let my tears flow freely
It's the house of love

What keeps our bond tight?
Character or chemistry
The answer is: Yes

It's good for our growth
We take monthly "fight-amins"
Our love gets stronger

Wow, you still want me
Despite my independence
You love my freedom

I'm a chameleon
Indian, Puerto Rican
Least that's what they think

Blessed scheduling
Able to have fun and work
Football and parties

Praying on the phone,
Without a doubt, strengthens us
In for the long haul

Like Amazing Grace
Our eyes were blind, now we see
Through Jesus' eyes

Once oblivious
Eyes attuned to things of God
Sight forever changed

Glad you understand
Importance of Christian men
For discipleship

Like a gardener
God's word prunes us here and there
They hurt but we grow

One day at a time
I must take these words to heart
Or I'll go crazy

Again we agree
The best tears flow in God's house
Refuge for the soul

Haiku of Love and War

Elyse Braxton

Our relationship
For Jesus to watch over
Placed at the altar

We are in accord
To give everything to God
He gave it to us

I'm very thankful
I have not gotten sick here
Hope it stays that way

If not for you dear
I'd hardly ever get mail
Or care packages

Not real lonely here
Because we're all held captive
I like deployment

I'm Miss Popular
The men gathered 'round
I took their vitals

Lent my stethoscope
So they could hear their heart sounds
Feel a nurse's touch

Cutting boards are done
I'm super proud of my work
I love my design

I lose track of time
As I'm hand sanding with love
The hard work pays off

Even when I'm mad
I've never stopped loving you
Doubt I ever will

Joy of the two-step
Dancing to George Strait at home
Heart and feet in sync

Yes I get lonely
No desire for romance
Unless it's from you

I still get crushes
As it occupies my mind
With someone to like

What works best for me
Giving my love to patients
Win-win overall

I know you love me
In every thought, word, and deed
Hope you feel it too

Yes, I'm impatient
I KNOW you are worth the wait
There's no one better

You're on the money
NO one will love me like you
Or even come close

Elyse Braxton — Haiku of Love and War

The trials of today
Testimony tomorrow
Lead more to Jesus

To serve along you
On a Christian mission trip
Love through hands and heart

With you by my side
I think we should runaway
Dodge the search party

Talk of servanthood
And leading those to the Lord
Can't contain myself

It is December
But it's different in Kuwait
Still warm and sunny

Still attainable
Get my New Year's body back
One day at a time

First and only cold
In this Kuwaiti winter
Healthy for this long

They clamor for me
Vying for my attention
Southeast Indians

Just like UPS
They will deliver for me
'Tis good to be brown

I feel out of touch
The world moves on, I'm stagnant
Well, that's deployment!

I might be in print
An issue of Desert Voice
SURE to be "famous"

I fell right asleep
After my first stint on nights
I got 5 hours

I'm up in bed now
Sniffling and writing haiku
Munching on mixed nuts

For me to shape up
I have to get to the gym
Not motivated

But I AM ready
To be an elf in the shop
To work on the wood

Sounds of a helo
Who are they? What do they have?
Hope they'll be okay

Witnessed more death here
Than at my home hospital
Tragic loss of life

Haiku of Love and War

Elyse Braxton

You say you'll chase me
To the ends of earth and back
Here's my location

They're mesmerizing
There's something about your eyes
I could stare for days

I'm feeling banished
Now I'll go to Camp Buehring
Not my decision

The timing is off
I wasn't supposed to leave
Until my crew left

Moving north shortly
For a "second" deployment
Attached to the first

Counting down the days
Although it's not set in stone
When they'll really go

Folks are stir crazy
As their deployment's ending
I'm staying by choice

I must pace myself
I still have a ways to go
Before I depart

Reading devotions
The scriptures know what is best
Can't handle the truth

Not supposed to be
I'm separating too soon
Life just isn't fair

Gone from my "family"
Christmas, New Years and birthday
Now it's with strangers

Hurry up and wait
Happening all over again
There's no direction

Friends saying goodbye
I'm really going to miss them
What's a girl to do?

Mutual missing
My nursing team and corps staff
There was true caring

He said he loved me
I'm sure it was as a friend
Don't love him that way

Even the scriptures
Remind me that this is good
God's timing is best

My mood improving
A great opportunity
Is how it's perceived

Haiku of Love and War

Elyse Braxton

I'm a hard-charger
Seeking to meet challenges
Proving unknown strength

New perspective
This is a great career move
How can I NOT go?

The way I see it
I might as well stay up there
It can't be that bad

I am reminded
When I am out of control
God means it for good

I must keep the faith
As my vision is narrow
God is all knowing

My mind is made up
I'll remain at Camp Buehring
Change is a good thing

Maybe I'm lazy
It is said haiku are hard
Just seventeen sounds

Uneventful night
The ER at Arifjan
Time went so slowly

Getting excited
Of the possibilities
Of moving up north

Wherever I go
Sunshine's bound to follow me
Self-manufactured

Learned on Saturday
The mission has been canceled
I might move later

Very selective
As to who enters my heart
My heart is your heart

Really kids at heart
Who pretend being grownups
Through words and actions

The belle of the ball
They came out of the woodwork
To ask me to dance

What attracted them?
Ugly Betty Navy Nurse
Probably my smile

We danced kind of close
Not emotionally attached
It was just dancing

I'm happy to stay
I would've missed my colleagues
They are family

Hugs of excitement
As I told them the good news
Not leaving them yet

I'd still like the chance
To try something different
To serve, learn, and grow

Daily devotions
Allow us to connect higher
With the True Source

Reading the scriptures
Gives us our daily advice
For Godly living

Can't imagine life
Without God, Jesus, and you
The loves of my life

Come Holy Spirit
Our hearts are a home for you
Have Your way with us

Going to Qatar
Give us traveling mercies
Thank you in advance

Teammates forever
We do what Jesus would do
God wrote the playbook

Unable to sleep
He asked me to talk to him
Take away his pain

Young soldier patients
Old enough to be their Mom
Yet they're my brothers

Set aside by God
To express His awesome love
For the world to see

Mighty thesaurus
A haiku artist's best friend
When help is needed

A burden lifted
Having Christian fellowship
What Jesus would do

Shared conversation
Jesus is the common link
Friendship grows stronger

Breaking up is hard
When we don't want to let go
As we are soulmates

You tell me I'm free
That I can meet other men
We're both very scared

I just close my eyes
Feeling the Latin rhythms
To my very soul

Haiku of Love and War

Even when confused
Your eyes remain so vivid
Unforgettable

The shy man approached
We chatted a bit last night
I'm building rapport

Constant rebuilding
Of our phone relationship
All we have right now

My thumb drive's broken
Admittedly I'm distraught
Hope they can fix it

My eyes remember
Equally my emotions
Can't recall your kiss

Deployment is hard
When you're not legally wed
No tie to bind me

It's getting harder
To keep the relationship
We've been gone so long

Can our love be saved?
With rekindled affection
We both sure hope so

I do not love him
But I sure am curious
As to who he is

Excitement last night
As we took down a patient
Adrenalin rush

I enjoy our chats
He reads devotions to me
I like to listen

I'm very confused
Don't want to hurt anyone
I want to know him

I feel like a fool
Giving you my love too soon
And my needs aren't met

You say you want me
Lately I find talk is cheap
Actions speak louder

It's the "world" in me
That gets me into trouble
God's the way to go

As the days move on
I think, "This was just a fling"
No destination

Doubts keep popping up
This relationship hassle
It's just not worth it

Haiku of Love and War

This isn't working
I'd prefer to be alone
Easier that way

Wheels are just spinning
Is this a waste of my time?
What's in it for me?

"It's all in God's time"
Is your latest patience "line"
Does it work for you?

Sorry you suffer
God is not punishing you
It's your decision

Ever in pursuit
The four corners of the globe
You will track me down

No comparison
Nor compatibility
Do the others have

I feel set aside
To love and be loved by you
The wait is so hard

Starting to forget
It's been more than five months now
What your kisses do

I miss your kisses
Our lips are jumper cables
To charge us back up

The final breakup
The romance has been removed
Yet the love remains

Ever the servant
I pray your needs will be met
I cannot meet them

Great pain in your voice
We both can't have what we want
Timing really stinks

Huge lump on my arm
From the anthrax injection
One more then I'm done!

When I'm down, you're up
And when I'm up, you are down
Seesaw of heartache

Here we go again
Adversity thus triumph
Friendship ever grows

Deep conversation
Sharing of our hearts and minds
Friendship grows deeper

I'm ever humbled
To be labeled a benchmark
A blessing and curse

Hard to keep it real
How can love and callings mix?
God has the answer

Heartbroken patient
Accepts my hands for a prayer
Sleeping in peace now

Back from the OR
He said I was a good nurse
Means ever so much

The art of nursing
Privileged intimacy
I get paid to love!

The power of touch
Conveys love, caring, support
To give and receive

Are you a doctor?
Nope, I'm better – I'm a nurse!
Love around the clock

Proud to be a nurse
Giving love at the bedside
We're not forgotten

The nurse and corps staff
No medals given, just praise
The silent heroes

Are you having pain?
How can I serve you better?
How do you feel now?

A celebrity
Recognized by our patients
For a job well done

She believes in me
That I'm a capable nurse
To take on new tasks

You're in great turmoil
Deep conversation with Mom
Held up inside you

Crying on the phone
Didn't know of your heartbreak
I can't read your mind

I have not a clue
The pain you are describing
Know I'm here for you

The blood of Jesus
Is a satan eraser
he has no power

You can't get enough
Reading and hearing the Word
Knowledge deepening

First Corinthians
Chapter 13 about Love
Your new favorite

Getting frustrated
I'm unable to connect
With free internet

You've found the secret
God's Word is a soothing balm
Apply heavily

Qatar

Our trip to Qatar
Lots of hurry up and wait
For our vacation

A foosball novice
I made some really nice plays
And mocked the Major

Finally got there
Exhausted on arrival
We went straight to bed

Was out way too late
They even called the MPs
Did the walk of shame

I had them worried
They didn't know where I was
And no phone number

Was perfectly safe
Spending time with a Christian
They really love me

Escape from the war
The apartment took me back
I was in the States!

Despite the concern
I raised, I have no regrets
I felt slightly free

I sensed some tension
I am not a mind reader
She is still upset

I thought we were cool
I asked for her forgiveness
I hope in due time

If you hold a grudge
You're incapable to hug
And it makes you frown

Really all my fault
I was inconsiderate
Selfish to the core

In Doha, Qatar
The strawberry hookah pipe
Made me hypoxic

The Four Season's lunch
Entertaining company
Wonderful buffet

Elyse Braxton — Haiku of Love and War

Walking in the Malls
The women dressed all in black
Don't make eye contact

Shopping for jewelry
Haggling is required
I gave it my best

A power shopper
Beautiful bangle for Mom
My mission complete

I'm thinking next time
I'll spend my 4 days on base
I've now seen Qatar

I enjoyed the time
However once is enough
Soon things will heat up

If I had a choice
I would go back to Landstuhl
For my 4-day pass

Army/Navy Game

Teasing the soldiers
With my Beat Army t-shirts
Pleasing my shipmates

Army/Navy game
I will be a cheerleader
Provided I'm off

Shirt taped to my blouse
Army taunting continues
But only at work

We are outnumbered
The Army is Goliath
Navy is David

I'm a cheerleader
For Navy's flag football team
Rah Rah Sis Boom Bah

We've got the spir-rit
For the Army/Navy game
At Camp Arifjan

It's almost game day
I hope I will get to cheer
Priceless adventure

I'm saving my voice
So I can cheer on game day
This is so much fun

I feel popular
Just the way cheerleaders do
All eyes were on us

Stand on the sideline
Keeping an eye on her crush
Secretly cheers him

All my trash talking
Was not in vain as we won
Officers, at least

Everyone loved us
Our halftime show was the best
Comments on my moves

Lights, camera, action
I turned it on for the crowd
I had so much fun!

A magical day
Army/Navy flag football
First here in Kuwait

In my cheering shirt
I love the recognition
Want to keep it on

We really did well
As we learned all those routines
In less than a week

Navy girl power
Officer and enlisted
It was just us girls

Incarceration
But that's what war does to you
Never thought I'd cheer

Is he watching her
As she cheers and struts her stuff?
She really hopes so

Almost 42
A cartwheel and a round-off
Got it going on!

We've got the spirit
Deployment like none other
A great time of year

In the name of fun
The compliments are flowing
People are so proud

Karaoke time
Instead of Navy football
Bonding with family

Army/Navy game
One of my favorite days
Unforgettable

Out of uniform
I got to dance and shake it
The real me came out

I thought I looked cute
All "roughneck" with my boots on
Yet girly above

Silent bragging rights
Navy won two out of three
I will be gracious

Glad the Navy won
Or Army would track me down
And get in MY face

The CO loved us
He wants us to dance again
For Christmas party

Christmas

Another routine
"Solid Blue and Gold" dancers
To dance for Christmas

Didn't like my name
"The Christmas Angel" dancers
Would be our title

Crowd loved us so much
Wanted repeat performance
We're celebrities!

Desert Wonderland
It's not the same without snow
But Jesus is here

Candlelight service
Carolers in uniform
Celebrate Jesus

We sang Silent Night
At the candlelight service
Didn't cry this time

Christmas in Kuwait
Crying sentimental tears
Over my stocking

Charged with emotion
First stocking I remember
A Mother's true love

Christmas opera
I open my gifts alone
Yet I am not sad

A Zone bar and juice
My Christmas breakfast in bed
Cozy little meal

My Christmas stocking
Hung on my "sheet door" with care
In it I got COAL!!!!

Munching on Chex Mix
But don't want crumbs in the bed
So I'm real careful

She's strong in her faith
But she feels she's backsliding
It's hard while deployed

We still have it good
Compared to the warriors
No need to complain

The holiday lull
There are even less patients
Calm before the storm

It's nice to have church
Talking about God's teachings
And our miracles

You know what's funny?
The more we acknowledge God
He blesses us more!

A surprise visit
To hug me, her special nurse
That's a day maker

Familiar faces
Our patients up and about
As we walk on base

Patients improving
On the road to true healing
Discharge paperwork!

Dinner and dancing
With the sweet Sergeant Major
He brought me a gift!

Well, it's New Year's Eve
No champagne or ball dropping
You're not here to kiss

The close of a year
Limerick for the log book
Navy tradition

Hidden in the back
I wished you Happy Birthday
I wouldn't forget

Just another day
Non-climactic New Year's Eve
Spent it on the phone

Start of the New Year
365 days
Where did the time go?

A simple "Thank you"
Gift of appreciation
Provides me favor

It is not often
That I'm quiet on the phone
You need to be heard

Haiku of Love and War

Elyse Braxton

New Wave deploying
Soon they'll be here in country
And we'll say goodbye

The poor newcomers
Without desert holidays
They're missing something

Ambitious soldier
I enjoy dancing with you
But you're way too young

Perception equals
Reality many times
Not fair, but it's true

A thirst for knowledge
Your voracious appetite
For the Bread of Life

As you are seeing
With deeper love for Jesus
Will come more attacks

Fear not, disciple
The Bible has equipped you
To fight and win

Two weeks away
I hope I'll be remembered
When it's my birthday

I get insecure
When I feel I'm forgotten
I want to matter

Reading devotions
Solidifies our friendship
Best part of the day

My desert birthday
Tears flowed over ice cream cake
I was deeply touched

Lunch with ER doc
Hit on by a contractor
42 is good!

I'm feeling the love
And am tooting my own horn
As it's my birthday

I miss human touch
I really want to snuggle
Need a warm body

Called up to the front
He didn't believe my age
Must I show ID?

The two birthday girls
Made to sing to each other
Then dance for the crowd

I'm building rapport
Getting to know folks better
Then they have to leave

I will walk with you
I find you mysterious
But you don't know that

Going to Buehring
The biggest question is "When?"
I'll do what I'm told

Hurry up and Wait
Evolution in patience
For military

Will someone hold me?
I'm not looking for a fling
I just want the touch

Human animal
Needs to be part of the pack
No self-reliance

Medevac to Landstuhl, Germany via Ali Al Salem AFB, Kuwait and Balad, Iraq

Back to my birthplace
A medevac to Landstuhl
Where this nurse was "born"

Medical escort
A free trip to Germany
Where it all started

Ali Al Salem
Holding ground for medevacs
Out to Germany

Air Force does it right
Comfortable amenities
Yet I'll stay Navy

Sharing a bedroom
A nightstand separates us
I'm your guardian

In the patient lounge
We're talking about Jesus
With my "family"

Landing in Balad
It's called "Mortar-itaville"
It's shelled every day

A mass casualty
Helos flying in injured
A frenetic pace

You're under my care
We joke about your lost hat
Try to meet your needs

Talk about divine
Doc let me go to Landstuhl
Rather than stay back

Patients on litters
We load on buses and planes
Our precious cargo

I worked my butt off
They needed more manpower
Such a joy to serve

The C-17
Carries patients and cargo
Ultra-versatile

Landed at Ramstein
And who is there to greet us?
A chaplain I know

I came full circle
My return trip to Landstuhl
Love and warriors

The commissary
Nothing but food and children
What a culture shock

Bought myself a rose
The beauty brought me to tears
Don't see flowers much

People in civies
More so than in uniform
A rare sight to see

Trees, grass, and mountains
No speck of desert in sight
Total eye candy

A slice of freedom
Each bite savored and treasured
If just for a while

Trip to Heidelberg
A divine invitation
From a church lady

On the Autobahn
We're happily having "church"
As cars speed along

It's not about me
I really wanted to stay
But I'm on the clock

Divine flight delay
Allowed me to see my friends
Without any guilt

Thank God for ear plugs
Those C-17's are loud!
And poorly heated

In the Armed Forces
There's no such thing as "on time"
True test of patience

Excitement junkie
They need nurses in Iraq?
I just want to grow!

I'm already here
New place and different job
I'd think about it

I've got the top bunk
No bed linens provided
It's not the Air Force

Slept through my alarm
I hardly got any sleep
I'll take the next bus

Camp Buehring

Back from Germany
Mad dash to pack up my things
I leave tomorrow

Giving hugs goodbye
To the folks at Arifjan
Trying not to cry

Can I sit with you?
I want to know you better
And you to know me

Excuse to hug you
As it's my last day on base
Hope we'll stay in touch

Don't want a boyfriend
I just want friends who are men
Different perspective

What is he thinking?
Is he attracted to me?
Could be a mirage

Riding in a van
My counterpart and I chat
We'll be a great team

Welcome to Buehring
Last stop before moving north
To fight for freedom

First day on the job
We had an air medevac
Great for first timers

Height of the trauma
I maintained my composure
Stated our Captain

Why am I a nurse?
My passion and compassion
The troops are my love

My reflective belt
Must be worn from 6 to 6
They're very strict here

Elyse Braxton — Haiku of Love and War

Our cozy clinic
With flags flying on the porch
All we need are rocking chairs.

In my little room
A temporary trailer
With bunks and lockers

The bathroom's outside
Shower stuff, makeup in hand
As I trudge half dressed

Goodbye open bay
15 bunk beds down each side
With quiet hours

No longer Ensign
Now Lieutenant Junior Grade
Got my silver bar!

The same time zone now
Harder to find privacy
When we're on the phone

I am still learning
But I can love like a champ
The art of nursing

Alone in my bunk
I get lonely when I'm bored
And have no purpose

Helos overhead
The rhythm of their rotors
Slicing through the air

Funny how one word
Can put progress in reverse
Here we go again

We live the tango
Constant pushing and pulling
Of tender heart strings

You are my best friend
Not my lover or husband
This has to suffice

Why do you still chase?
You ever think about me
And how I'm feeling?

Reprogram myself
To treat you like a brother
No romance in sight

Soldiers everywhere
With M16s on their back
Now, it's for practice

I must improvise
Computers are down, no help
I'll use what I have

A big task at hand
To immunize all the troops
Before advancing

Haiku of Love and War

Understanding now
Why woman is made for man
They really need us

Yet it's opposite
Man wasn't made for woman
Wonder why that is?

What is the story?
Are women self-sufficient?
So they don't need men

Oh Heaven help me!
I'm lonely and impatient
Jesus, take me NOW!

On the learning curve
These boots are made for climbing
I'll reach the summit

Calm before the storm
A surge will be here shortly
We'll be fully trained

The constant sandstorms
Were extremely annoying
Could have been worse though

Sandstorm is blowing
Reminds me of a blizzard
Both require boots

The hazy brown sky
Wind blowing my cover off
Sand grit in my teeth

The sand is so fine
Triggered the smoke detector
Removed battery

I'm close but distant
You're always in pursuit mode
Don't understand you

Sparkles on the floor
From my gift's wrapping paper
They're hard to clean up

Such a thoughtful friend
She remembered my birthday
Constant surprises

The Internet's down
They say for two weeks or so
THIS is roughing it!

As an Officer
I make decisions and lead
Thinking of my troops

Lead by example
I can roll up my sleeves too
We'll share in the dirt

TCN Ladies
Bangladeshi, Sri Lankan
Work hard for the dough

Haiku of Love and War

Been here for a week
Pork on the menu four times
For lunch and dinner

The other white meat
I sure miss thin crust pizza
With red pepper flakes

The smell of the sand
Feel like I'm always dirty
How do my lungs look?

The loneliness breaks
Just after Valentine's Day
For deployed singles

My lonely heart cure:
Sending Valentine's Day cards
To single girl friends

I long to salsa
Partnering up and touching
Soul stirring rhythms

I dropped all those hints
Yes, I was disappointed
No birthday wishes

I'm done romancing
We're strictly down to friendship
Don't want to kiss you

Feel like I am air
Something you depend upon
For your survival

I don't hold my breath
As in "Waiting to Exhale"
I will live and breathe

I'll accept your gifts
As I do from the others
They all weigh the same

Think my heart's shut down
It's been given out so much
But to the wrong ones

My heart's with Jesus
I know He'll guard it safely
Handle it with care

I long to be known
And loved by a single man
Who loves Jesus Christ

If I want a fling
I know just the man to call
But it's not worth it

A cable was cut
Internet's down all over
How will we survive?!

Can't say I love you
At least not romantically
But we'll still be friends

After this go-round
I'll be ready to go home
Some won't have that chance

Leadership secret:
Have them want to work for you
Thanks and praise go far

I long to be held
I'd jump at anyone now
I really miss touch

Taking smaller steps
In this marathon friendship
We will persevere

Just out of the blue
I was minding my business
A soldier says, "Hi"

My anthrax party
172
Injections given

Deployed Super Bowl
They don't play the commercials
Armed Forces Network

Cell phone doesn't work
SIM card is compatible
Can't get a signal

Familiar faces
My patients from Arifjan
Who are stationed here

I should watch my mouth
Might say something I'll regret
And hurt your feelings

Homesick for dancing
I miss that from Arifjan
Not much to do here

Combat boots so tight
Calves look like link sausages
When the day is done

You say you're lonely
Yet you've got somewhere to go
I'm all by myself!

Don't really need you
The way you depend on me
I get no reward

Borderline clingy
You're not truly desperate
But you can't let go

Deployment is rough
Takes a toll on my body
Short on affection

This is not healthy
The timing's never been right
Starting to lose faith

Elyse Braxton — Haiku of Love and War

It's unnatural
To go without human touch
I'm going crazy!

Who can I run to?
For some big comforting hugs
Mom's so far away

Now you're my brother
We can't go "lower" than this
I'll still stay in touch

None of our efforts
Were in vain because we loved
Each other fully

We can only hope
Love is like riding a bike
We'll never forget

The film "The Notebook"
A fictitious love story
Ours is non-fiction

I will keep writing
Catharsis for my feelings
It helps me to cope

The perfect person
Extremely compatible
Imperfect timing

Unlike the others
Your gifts aren't disposable
They're for my hope chest

My sibling in Christ
We encourage and support
Each other in prayer

Blessed reliance
For Jesus to heal our hurts
Makes us grow stronger

Pain, strain, and struggle
Suffering brings victory
Our faith is tested

Chewed out yesterday
Failure to communicate
It happens sometime

I'm glad I'm secure
I can take what I'm given
Rolls right off my back

Nurses - made not born
Doctors, please don't forget that
You are just the same

Hard to be hands off
I like to jump in feet first
But I'm a leader

Guiding my Corpsmen
I have them practice with me
Then to the patient

Leaders are teachers
We guide and direct our class
To improve their skills

As an Officer
It's my job to take the hit
To protect my troops

To be called "L.T."
Is a sign of affection
"Ensign" was last month

God is a big God
He can take it when you're mad
It shows you trust Him

Praying for rebirth
Phoenix rose up from the flames
Lay it at the cross

This is a growth phase
Necessary solo trip
We will not lose touch

Although we're alone
We have Jesus' promises
For purest comfort

We're both struggling
But in different ways I'm sure
Give it to Jesus

Not even thirty
He has major eyelashes
Is there attraction?

He asked me my name
And if he could call me that
I think he likes me

Paged when I'm asleep
We couldn't get his IV
It took 7 sticks

I'm thanking the Lord
Love being a Nurse leader
In our clinic home

You just won't give up
Seems you'll never let me go
Day by day we pray

Is it really true
They don't think they'll make it home?
Wow, a soldier's mind

A girl-to-girl talk
Senior Chief's lessons on life
What an influence

So many buttocks
The IM injection queen
And so little time

Getting cynical
Witnessing stupidity
In the common man

Haiku of Love and War

Elyse Braxton

Internet's back up!
Connected to home again
We were so deprived

Chow hall lines are long
You can mail me cereal
So I can still eat

Once the surge hits us
We'll eat, sleep, and drink the troops
And then they'll be off

Now that I'm awake
Alert and oriented
I will write haiku

Gave gloves off my hands
To keep the housekeeper warm
More gloves in my room

Can't remember when
I last looked at your picture
Went straight to your eyes

Five providers now
Yet there'll be no more nurses
We won't get a break

Tons of enlisted
Starting to get in my way
I might step on one

I'm loving my job
Leadership at this level
Almost unheard of

Chance of a lifetime
This back-to-back deployment
I'll be bored at home

Right on the money
Why the medic hangs with us:
The pretty young girls!

Familiar faces
Once patients at Arifjan
Are all better here

For next 4-day pass
Hope to do a medevac
Working vacation

Savored the freedom
When I went to Germany
So many choices!

Fuzzy cream blanket
After washing, it STILL sheds
It stays in Kuwait

New Officers came
The two females live next door
I don't have to share

Still sleeping in bunks
We'll move to the trailer park
We are living large

Elyse Braxton — Haiku of Love and War

A familiar nurse
Gave me a hug and a lift
When he visited

Someday to Iraq
Navy medicine will move
We just don't know when

Got a care package
With chocolate covered pretzels
Gave up sweets for Lent ☹

Think I've changed my mind
I'd love to hold and kiss you
It's been a long time

Teachable moments
Had a patient with chest pain
Great for the Corpsmen

Improved programming
Will make entry much faster
For mass injections

A sense of humor
I don't leave home without it
Patients like it too

New sheriff in town
When Echo Wave 2 departs
Set up Foxtrot shop

Safety concerns here
Sexual assault rising
By the warriors

Not used to splurging
I'm conscious about money
SOME would say I'm "cheap"

Found the Mardi Gras
It was nothing but hip hop
Where was the salsa?

Know what I find odd?
Men will dance with each other
In the combat zone

Teaching the Corpsmen
I helped them with ECG's
Smart with the placement

She said I had guns
That my arms were muscular
That I must work out

Goodbye duty phone
THAT is a killer schedule
It's temporary

Reading Fern Michaels
I'm not used to non-fiction
Keeps my attention

Feeling slightly blah
Garlic pills and orange juice
Come to my rescue

Haiku of Love and War

A constant patient
Kept his word, brought in donuts
We'd been requesting

I miss healthful food
Soymilk, fiber, and couscous
Calorie control

Up at 5:30
To learn to drive in Kuwait
Things I do for love

I'm afraid to drive
The Kuwaitis are reckless
I don't want to die

Sunday afternoon
On my bunk in my undies
Really chilling out

Screening the patients
Shadowing a great doctor
Thanking God again

Feeling of pure bliss
Wearing a new pair of socks
My feet are smiling

Might be a 'J.G.'
You don't intimidate me
Because you're a doc

You may outrank me
But I am older than you
I will not crumble

You think you're so tough
Do you know who you're bossing?
I can hold my own

Turned on my cell phone
Most of the texts are from you
My heart is smiling

Dance lessons today
Salsa for Kansas soldiers
In my happy place

I've always loved you
No matter how much I fight
You have won my heart

Single girls did it
We survived Valentine's Day!!!
Peace till Thanksgiving

My age means wisdom
I can tell by your giggles
You feel insecure

Paperwork's complete
For my trip to Australia
A free vacation

In the trailer park
I have a room of my own
For the next five months

Life of luxury
Fridge, TV, and DVD
Lots of furniture

Amazing Corpsmen
They giggle while they're learning
Truly quick studies

The blinding dust storms
Grit in your eyes, ears, and mouth
Covers EVERYthing!

Back to Arifjan
Haircut, errands, and shopping
Small taste of freedom

Walking in AJ
A former patient stopped me
Nice he remembered

We had a trauma
As prepared as we could be
He was stabilized

Tension in the ranks
Women, power, and status
Glad I'm not in it

Sensitive egos
Come on now – it's the mission
Grow up already!

You MUST be crazy
To pull the integral man
We're lost without him

We had a rough spot
We seem to be on track now
Happy together

New dance, same partner
I've never stopped loving you
In for the long haul

Our friendship growing
Jesus is our foundation
As He's always been

Boxes everywhere
Major accumulation
In my desert home

My sense of humor
And genuine caring
Perfect for nursing

Having good manners
Like saying "Thank you" and "Please"
Can work miracles

Let my character
Speak for itself, when I can't
As I am junior

I'll see you next year
We'll catch up and talk all night
Dance and be goofy

Haiku of Love and War

Elyse Braxton

Easy to let go
Beloved rank of Ensign
Now I'm called, "L.T."

Don't want to believe
Everyone's a backstabber
To advance in rank

No potty mouth here
I don't swear like a Sailor
Although I am one

All volunteer force
Next greatest generation
Dad truly believes

Two more females here
They outrank me by a mile
I stay to myself

The eager Corpsmen
Place IV's in each other
For practice and fun

I had my hair down
The day I got my haircut
Rapunzel action

Not much to do here
So I read and grow my hair
Hang out with our staff

Big box to mail home
This is just for starters too
I've got so much stuff!

My next deployment?
JUST the bare necessities
Clothes and computer

Still really cold out
It might be warmer stateside
Highs in the 50's

Little courtesies
Are paying big dividends
When you're out in town

Love my enemies
And deal with persecution
It's STILL not the Cross

One day at a time
Starting my fitness routine
On the road to health

The closing prayer
Had me crying in my seat
He spoke of my pain

He has given us
Daily bread for consumption
We're never at want

How can I serve you?
Be an instrument of love?
I'm here and able

Oh, Heaven help me
I can't do anything right
It seems, in their eyes

Flamenco music
Emotions "said" without words
It's universal

On a shopping spree
Jewelry and a camera
Possibly a watch

I am laying low
Letting Dad be with his thoughts
He needs time to think

Beautiful spirit
There is a joy about you
You must go to church

Survived this last week
I didn't get "beaten up"
I still pray for them

Gift of cereal
From a Special Forces guy
New admirer

Hopes are feeling dashed
Are you coming to see me?
Getting impatient

Nothing but fried food
Or at least that's what it seems
For the duty crew

Really bare bones here
Very few DSN phones
For fifty people

To the moon she'll go
My ambitious trailer mate
That would be so cool

Every step in place
Working on her childhood dream
Astronaut Tanya

Constant state of thanks
Lifetime opportunities
Only at Buehring

In the trauma class
The mannequins squirted blood
It looked like fruit punch

Mass casualty drill
And what beautiful weather
It was for practice

Dancing in my room
Imaginary two-step
I wish you were here

I like the ER
Mostly the hands-on aspect
And variety

Haiku of Love and War

Elyse Braxton

It was worth the hike
To have some Indian food
It was just perfect

Sick call screener's course
On abdomen and rectum
I say "Guts and Butts"

I enjoy teaching
As I train up our Corpsmen
They are our future

I can't remember
What it's like to be 19
The joys and the fears

You're praying out loud
Within your devotion group
In the cool morning

He named me "Hanan"
Meaning mercy, compassion
An Arabic "gift"

Speaking Arabic
Just the smallest of phrases
Makes their eyes light up

An invitation
To dine with the Kuwaitis
I hope we're allowed

Focus on Jesus
Will help us endure all things
Until it's our time

The virtues of Ruth
A biblical role-model
For all womankind

Rachel and Jacob
Fourteen years he served for her
A blink of an eye

I found some soy milk!
They're gearing up for the surge
They heard my request?

Not much to do here
For forms of entertainment
As it's transient

At a healthy weight
Just want my old clothes to fit
And thus save money

Familiar faces
I say, "repeat offenders"
Beloved patients

It's all about "free"
Greeting cards, devotionals
Support for the troops

I found a hookup
Commissary in Riyadh
To mail food items

Elyse Braxton Haiku of Love and War

Small care packages
Scavenged, re-gifted or made
They're loaded with love

Her mission complete
Her Mom has six months to live
I'm her mother's age

I can't imagine
To lose a parent so young
Both in their young prime

Feeling downhearted
My character was attacked
Personal Judas

Came back to my room
And read the scriptures out loud
Prayers for enemy

God you know my heart
I want to follow Your will
I submit to You

What a nice surprise
Happy desert reunion
Big Daddy Carlos

Walking from Sick Call
A soldier walks towards me
It's you! Really you!!!!

We parted our ways
New Year's Two thousand three
And now face to face

Have a new photo
For your Mom's little café
Us here in Buerhing

Everywhere I look
I see 4th ID patches
Happy reminders

What a happy day
Long distance friends reunite
For a brief moment

I saw her today
Patriotic spokesmodel
Deployed amputee

She could have stayed home
She already gave her leg
She's Active Duty

I want to know her
SEALs, Marines, special ops - no
SHE's the toughest "guy"

The bravest alive
Wears a bra, totes a rifle
Walks with prosthetics

Church on Good Friday
Chapel full of Godly men
Singing their hearts out

The sunrise service
Worshipping our risen Lord
Resurrection Day

First Easter Egg Hunt
In my uniform and boots
Scrambling in the heat

Now that I'm away
Miss Mom's potato salad
With Easter dinner

Beauty of Easter
Praise the Lord; He has risen
Rejoice and be glad

A little rough spot
A spiritual attack
But we're stronger now

I had forgotten
Growth makes us vulnerable
To things not of God

Two are pretty strong
Add the Holy Trinity
Nothing's mightier

We met that hurdle
Only by the grace of God
Now we soar with joy

Constantly growing
Clinical skills improving
I am right on track

God give me the strength
To always submit to You
As You know what's best

Deeper in scripture
Our devotional hour
Highlight of our day

From all walks of life
One thing we have in common
We defend freedom

The soldier broke down
As he can't leave with his troops
We'll take care of him

Someone to talk to
A tissue, comforting word
Ever so grateful

The Army loves us
Because of care we provide
Day in and day out

Great minds think alike
I trust you implicitly
You are my best friend

You are on fire
Your passion burns fervently
As your faith deepens

I want to serve You
Lord, what is it that I'm to do?
Have to share my love

There is less tension
I pray for my enemies
That they know Your love

Reading the scriptures
Your love is on every page
Satisfies my soul

With divine timing
Care packages full of food
Goodbye chow hall lines

The loves of my life
It is all about the troops
They inspire me

I am not perfect
But I seek to be God-like
In a human form

With eyes of wisdom
Only from experience
Can I see deeper

Uplifting music
Songs of love to Jesus Christ
And God, the Father

I rode a camel!
Had to while it was still cool
For Kuwait weather

You see what I can't
I value your opinion
I know you mean well

Heightened stress levels
I have never cried so much
It's cumulative

Have to take a break
For me and my mental health
I'm burning out fast

My cell phone in hand
Reading your text messages
Smile and remember

Thought I had control
Might have been my perception
Guess that's how I coped

Lord teach us to love
With purity and patience
Without conditions

Father cleanse our eyes
Give us sensitivity
Improve our vision

Give me the insight
To see what Jesus would see
And do what He'd do

My heart is open
This is your new residence
I'll give you the tour

The cliché is right
To know You is to love You
'Cause You loved us first

Not much to do here
When I said, "I grow my hair"
I wasn't kidding

A field exercise
Bread of life and the Bible
Our survival kit

Isn't love the best?
Puts a smile on face and heart
That the world can see

Heard in our voices
The sheer joy of each other
Whether near or far

A mental health day
Being granted some time off
I'm a new woman

Divine solitude
Even Jesus needed time
To spend by himself

My tank was empty
I had time to charge back up
I can give again

Memories from music
As if they were yesterday
Our playlists of love

Not an easy life
Delayed gratification
But it's well worth it

Words of eloquence
Describe your heartfelt feelings
In a prayer to God

Small finds here and there
Our desert care packages
Creative gifting

Crying on the phone
I could not make sentences
I was so stressed out

Help me Father God
How can I serve your children?
You're all that matters

I truly believe
In divine inspiration
That's why I'm a nurse

Life experience
Something that money can't buy
It is gained daily

Haiku of Love and War

Elyse Braxton

The eyes of wisdom
Combined with youthful spirit
Together, perfect

Locked up in my room
Playing music and movies
I wish you were here

It was my first time
To use a surgical blade
But he didn't know

Only afterwards
Did I share with the patient
That he was my first

Heat casualty time
Have rectal thermometer
And I will travel

The heat's upon us
Temps now at 100
Please stay hydrated

A day just for me
Music, haiku, and movies
Much needed down time

Was told to slow down
No need to rush my career
Take it day by day

You know what I dream?
To be a beautiful bride
Youthful as ever

Mmmm, those eyes of yours
I keep getting lost in them
Call off the search crew

Still don't understand
How you can go on loving
While I'm fighting you

I really do though
It's simply the God in you
Loving God in me

And after all this
You still think I am perfect
I will not argue

Seriously though
I am in a state of thanks
For your and God's love

The maintenance men
Are working on a light bulb
Taking forever

I'm not complaining
It is giving me a break
To write more haiku

I'm writing again
My emotions are flowing
Back in the saddle

Met with the Chaplain
Seems they were really concerned
Came here just for me

It was Chaps' birthday
Got stranded by the sandstorm
Threw him a party

Return to Arifjan

Tensions on the job
I'm now back at Arifjan
It's all for the best

Not my decision
Administrative changes
Back to the "city"

First it was too late
To make changes to the teams
But it wasn't so

Moving like lightening
It was decided I'd go
But now I'm at peace

I feel out of place
I miss the hospital tent
This new place is huge!

A berthing uproar
Two nurses will have to share
I get a single

I'm easy going
I was patient with the move
Not the higher-ups

On the patio
I learned to play dominoes
I was home again

Hugs from Latinos
They were happy I was back
I missed this time too

The joy of dancing
It had been such a long time
That I'd beamed this much

I don't understand
How people can hate so much
Or at least despise

The sermon at church
Talked of suffering for Christ
I sure have lately

It is the Bible
That provides salve to my scars
To ensure healing

When you attack me
It shows you are insecure
I will pray for you

Seems there was a fight
The girls didn't want to move
But I outrank them

Easy to find joy
I just need to think of you
As I praise Jesus

I'm in constant praise
For the blessings God's bestowed
Known or unrevealed

Singing songs of praise
Brings blissful joy to my heart
The lyrics ring true

 fought and struggled
To be in control, not God
With God, I'm at peace

Everything I see
Hear or do, I want to share
These moments with you

As I grow in faith
I know God is in control
And that's a good thing

God is in control
There have been times I fought Him
But He always wins

How do I love thee?
It is rather effortless
You are my soulmate

To look in your eyes
I long to get lost in them
Can't take them off you

My hands brush your face
They lovingly caress your
Eyes, nose, cheeks, and lips

There is one thing though
About open bay berthing
It's freezing in here!

Feeling overwhelmed
As I try to find my way
In the hospital

My preceptor Sue
Is older and a mother
I'm very thankful

Longing for the tents
I miss the intimacy
Of our little space

Now it's all high tech
TVs at every bedside
Even have call bells

There's not much to do
When the workday is over
I miss Camp Buehring

Time goes so slowly
I am aging in reverse
I'm lonely and bored

I have been sheltered
I'm in a "safe" combat zone
Not truly fear-filled

How do they manage
When there are mortar attacks?
They keep moving on

Several have noticed
That my feathers don't ruffle
When stuff hits the fan

Thoughts of Bethesda
And the wounded warriors
Such sacrifices

Confidence growing
A knowledge base to build on
Feeling more seasoned

I'm in constant praise
Of the blessings God's bestowed
Known or unrevealed

Singing songs of praise
Brings blissful joy to my heart
The lyrics ring true

I'm her new best friend
As I provided pain meds
She wanted to die

Que sera sera
What does God have planned for me?
It's all a surprise

I've got the munchies
It's mostly due to boredom
Even past midnight

Military life
People constantly moving
Just more folks to love

I'm highly thought of
Because I'm an advocate
And I love my job

I don't know combat
And the fears they face daily
They must be on edge

Bless the warrior
During the mission at hand
Come home in one piece

Back in the woodshop
Flattered I was remembered
'Twas good to be home

It doesn't matter
How far we're separated
Bible keeps us close

Starting already
I've got a warrior's tan
Hands darker than arms

The new hospital
Is overwhelmingly large
I sure miss the tents

His inspired Words
The Bible is the handbook
To live a good life

In war zone churches
A large male congregation
Not so much stateside

Oh Father, thank you
For heaping blessings on me
I can't hold them all!

Never more patient
As I have faith in You, God
You're always on time

Songs of love and praise
Silently sung in our heads
Twenty-four seven

The Bible's alive
Two thousand years of the truth
Direction and love

Trying to fit in
As I am new to the Det
Yet old in Kuwait

Under the radar
Because many don't know me
I find that perfect

I'm glad I'm secure
Since I am the foreigner
To this new "culture"

Under construction
Aquatic desires dry
But not forever

I will get to swim
During my time in Qatar
I sure miss chlorine

To put on muscle
And lose adipose tissue
Attainable goals

Qatar, again

More favor's revealed
Check-in time is earlier
For the 4-day pass

I took the last bus
So I had a shorter wait
To get to Qatar

With one hour less
For required check-in time
A five-hour wait

I marvel at God
In how obedience pays
Out huge dividends

My flight is delayed
I get to stay overnight
It ain't the Hilton

A former patient
Offered to carry my bags
How could I say no?

Much to my surprise
There's a pillow and a blanket
But the lights stayed on

I pretend to sleep
Bless my sleep shades and ear plugs
They're a true Godsend

As I walked around
I hear the Latin music
Salsa in Ali

I asked the first man
I saw if he'd dance with me
I'm glad he said yes

At my next briefing
My medevac patient's here!
Greet him with a hug

For a second time
A soldier carries my bags
Nursing's where it's at

Almost an hour
Has passed for our boarding time
But that's typical

We met by the sinks
We were both going to church
A new friend is made

More church at Chili's
I reflected on tithing
And how I've been blessed

A true act of faith
I can't afford NOT to tithe
God's richly blessed me

Everything joyful
I want to share it with you
Whether big or small

A three beer limit
However you pay for them
I didn't know that

Dinner with new friends
We're sharing food and laughter
Making memories

I'm the Desert Queen
Describing the glow belt sash
I'd wear at Buehring

In the USO
You have to take your shoes off
To keep the floor clean

In Arabic style
They have pillows on the floor
So you can lie down

Lying on the floor
Felt like I was in college
Watching dumb movies

A simple, "Shukran"
Provided me royal treatment
By the Generals

Falcon on my arm
Such a beautiful hunter
A rare treat indeed

In their meeting room
Eighteenth century paintings
Beloved Venice

Sweets and sweets galore
Presented in gold and blue
Money no object

Jet skis, ATVs
Deep sea fishing and free drinks
And they served camel!

Camel was tasty
It reminded me of lamb
Minus mint jelly

My newest 'uncles'
One and two-star Generals
Again, only me

Handsome Staff Sergeant
He's a cutie in her eyes
Yet it's me he likes

He's not my soul mate
Nor is he an Officer
I would be at fault

I'm truly flattered
That he's attracted to me
We have no future

Taught him to salsa
Turns out he's a quick study
Selfish dancing gain

A combat takeoff
Puts your stomach in your throat
And our stuff takes flight

Spring

My heart longs for you
When will I see you again?
Soon is far too late

Burning desires
To be in each other's arms
You're my one true love

He has HIV
He seemed to take the news well
I will pray for him

He's just a patient
Nothing to be afraid of
Meds will help a lot

Who are we to judge?
We are just as imperfect
As the other guy

We were shaken up
He's HIV positive
And such a young man

I would get the chills
His life has taken a turn
Moment to reflect

Ever so grateful
He thanked us for what we do
We get paid to love

He's not a leper
He's treated with dignity
Like everyone else

Modern medicine
Can halt the disease process
But not erase it

Reflections of life
It can be taken so fast
We must treasure it

Armed with the Bible
There's nothing we can't handle
When satan attacks

Love for enlisted
They are truly our backbone
Thus our greatest strength

We'll give God our plans
And He will direct our steps
To divine purpose

He's a temptation
The interested soldier
Have eyes of boredom

I saw him today
My northern persecutor
Felt nothing but peace

Haiku of Love and War

Elyse Braxton

The Nurse Corps leaders
Brought me back for my own good
Glad for protection

Walking to salsa
Saw Sergeant Major Buddy
He's in shy pursuit

It's funny with rank
We never use our first names
As I outrank him

Men in pursuit mode
They can be so attentive
I eat it all up!

I'm nine months complete
I've maintained a steady pace
Three more months to go

My heart's full of joy
I'm ridiculously in love
Whether near or far

It doesn't matter
How far we're separated
Bible keeps us close

Off to Australia
Soon I'll have my R&R
In two months I'm home!

I can't believe it
I'm three fourths of the way through
Steady as she goes

Senior was shipped out
Will she be "mission complete"?
I know she hopes not

Staff Sergeant in town
Was here to pick up supplies
I tried to help him

I know his partner
We're USO volunteers
They wanted to stay

No room at my inn
But there was room in Zone 6
They would sleep in tents

Tried to hook them up
With linen and toiletries
Instead they drove home

It seems sometime soon
There'll be a mass exodus
Of troops heading home

I'm not resting though
Most vacancies will be filled
'Least I would assume

Three more months to go
I'm sure the time will fly by
I go day by day

I think there is peace
With the nurse who had to move
Haven't felt ill will

To be a Christian
Means we'll be misunderstood
By non-believers

Goodies from my Mom
Oatmeal cookies and muffins
They survived the trip!

It's not easy God
I want to follow my will
Although it's unknown

We were number two
In the merengue contest
And we'll get trophies!!!

Our names were announced
My jaw dropped straight to the floor
We came in second!

We had never met
And you needed a partner
I stepped to the plate

I wanted to talk
Get to know his dancing style
I pulled out the stops

Yes, I danced closely
This was a competition
But the crowd loved it

What I find funny
Is that I had no feelings
It was just dancing

If WE were partners
They would see our chemistry
Whole 'nuther story

What was it they saw?
Not that I doubt the judges
I'm just curious

Wasn't my outfit
Unless PT gear and shoes
Was a fashion trend

Loved in two places
I'm really missed at Buehring
Majorly humbled

Corpsman had my back
When I was against the wall
More favor granted

Manic Depressive
Compliant to my limits
Still gotta watch her

Heightened frustration
Didn't have much sympathy
Brought it on herself

Elyse Braxton — Haiku of Love and War

Many find it hard
To deal with mental illness
It's lack of rapport

Seems I made a mark
In the hearts of the Corpsmen
They say they miss me

I get to give hugs
They happily hug me back
Sincere affection

Being a "mustang"
The enlisted respect me
I once wore their boots

I'm so full of joy
Everything's right in my world
For God made it so

My growing patience
Surprises me most of all
A gentle knowing

What a life I've lead
Can't say it's been a dull one
Adventures galore

Hope I can worship
If there's a small patient load
Great start to the week

Single and content
I thought to myself today
On my walk to work

Again God's favor
Record cool temperatures
While I'm in Kuwait

Not that it is cold
It's just not super hot yet
As it should be now

It is not my genes
But God who's my beautician
Of mind, body, soul

My eyes are changing
I need to stretch out my arms
To read the small print

It is okay though
That's what's supposed to happen
When we age with grace

I'm eating junk food
'Cause it's in front of my face
Must keep working out

I'm a newcomer
To the Foxtrot Detachment
But not out of place

I am self-contained
A social hermit I am
I enjoy myself

I don't feel left out
Because I'm new on the block
The kids play with me

Counting down to Oz
I'm going to Australia!
Getting excited!!!

Frequent Flyer Miles
I hope I'm eligible
With my free ticket

Dubai to Brisbane
It's a sixteen-hour flight
Pray for a good seat

Calves are killing me!
Buildup of lactic acid
From three days ago

Walking is painful
Doing the stairs is the worst
But I must go on

To reduce the pain
I need to stretch really well
And go for a jog

I will press on though
Tonight is Latin dancing
I teach basic steps

I received a rose!
A Mother's Day gift from church
Gave it to a Mom

Scrap wood serving boards
Similar to fingerprints
No two are alike

Heavenly Father
I'm humbled by your favor
You have blessed me so

Latin addiction
I want to master the steps
Feeling of success

The rhythms touch me
My body keeps moving but
I'm rather aloof

The ARCENT fun run
Had nothing fun about it
When mandatory

Up at four thirty
To muster at 5 am
Run at zero-6

In our PT gear
With the pomp and circumstance
Lined in formation

Six people across
Designed 18 people deep
We ran as a group

With flags and guidons
We ran and sang in cadence
Truly Navy strong

A nine-minute mile
Is the goal they set for us
We ran for a while

It was over 2
Miles for the run this morning
Happy I finished

After a while though
It was either run or sing
I couldn't do both

In the hospital
The ER was wall to wall
With Soldiers, of course

We've now been informed
The fun runs will be monthly
Pray I'll be on leave

Felt it in my calves
As we were chugging along
Hope I'll heal quickly

Navy Nurse Corps Centennial

The Navy Nurse Corps
Our Excellentenial
We've come a long way

Nurse Corps track relay
I did 6.25 miles!
Not terribly sore

Most I've run all year
The DNS was impressed
Didn't need O2

13 May '08
One hundred years of loving
The Navy Nurse Corps

Water pistol fights
Were breaking out all over
At the Nurse Corps Ball

It didn't matter
Strangers were shooting at strangers
We were all fair game

Plastic soldiers and snakes
Placed in the open sand bags
As decorations

Camouflage netting
For unique table runners
Clever idea

To "Ice Ice Baby"
DFA and Master Chief
Danced like Kid and Play

For Soul Train Lineup
I grabbed Jones to dance the bump
The crowd cheered us on

Line dancing time
Come on show us what you got!
Shake it, don't break it!

The photographer
Should be in FRONT of the lens
That boy is gorgeous!

Is he a model?
If not, he really should be
Tall, nice, and handsome

Let the music play
I can dance the night away
Must it end early?

Efforts not in vain
The DJ played some salsa
And asked me to dance

The solo couple
Dancing to a bachata
As they're cleaning up

Perfect Nurse Corps Ball
Relaxed family having fun
No formality

Even our Captain
Got into the water fun
Too scared to shoot her

The water pistols
Reminded us of childhood
Smiles, fun, and laughter

Universal theme
Green toy soldiers and pistols
War is around us

So much Nurse Corps pride
We have come such a long way
We're far from over

100th Birthday
Nurse Corps "born" today
Lookin' good baby!

The Sacred Twenty
Trailblazers in their own right
Bet they're proud of us

The Navy's finest
We say, "I'm a Navy Nurse"
And we're proud to serve

R&R to Oz

I'm Australia bound
Lifetime opportunity
Because of the war

Haiku of Love and War

Elyse Braxton

A chance encounter
Led to church over dinner
With stranger now friend

I felt rather odd
In Kuwait City airport
So many Arabs

Looking like angels
In hats and white "man-dresses"
Kuwaitis flutter

An endless buffet
Pigging out on airplane food
It's not what I'm used to

Landing in Dubai
The humidity kissed me
And tousled my hair

Interesting skylines
Unlike those I've seen stateside
They're ultra-modern

Halfway to Brisbane
First we'll stop in Singapore
Then less than halfway

Twenty-four hundred
Dollars for my plane ticket
Cost me six months work!

So many places
I would like us to visit
The travel mag's fault

Trying to adjust
To my upcoming time zone
Hope I'll fall asleep

I've been up since four
Thirty yesterday morning
For my R&R

Two former Cadets
Are both stationed in Balad
Delayed honeymoon

Nose and toes are numb
Because of the chardonnay
And high altitude

I'm feeling giddy
The wine's intoxicating
No one to laugh with

Not used to drinking
I am super sensitive
To the alcohol

I'm a happy drunk
If you could even say that
Hope I fall asleep

Yeah, my lips are numb
My whole body's feeling it
I'm such a lightweight

Haiku of Love and War

Elyse Braxton

Playful little boy
Sitting in the row with me
I hope he's quiet

Nap interrupted
When they bang my sleep pillow
As they walk about

Landed in Brisbane
Greeted by "Aunt" and "Uncle"
Boy did they have plans

Christian fellowship
Served with a potluck dinner
Always praising God

Spending time with kids
Keisha made herself at home
Lounging up on me

Clouds, so many clouds
Beautiful fluffy goodness
Against the blue sky

There is a drought here
It's lush compared to Kuwait
Awesome greenery

It's so delicious
15-day taste of freedom
Two months, I'll be home!

I miss solitude
To type on the computer
Thus written haiku

Don't want to intrude
Don't want to upset their routine
Don't want a schedule

Two little Maltese
Tiny Powder and Satchmo
The barking slippers

The cry of babies
A sound I don't often hear
It was kind of nice

Not in uniform
As I worshipped this morning
Took getting used to

Much colder in Oz
Compared to my desert home
My body is homesick

It will get colder
The further south I explore
Here in Australia

I think I will splurge
And reserve a hotel room
When I'm in Sydney

Own bed and bathroom
I'll have the heat turned on high
But no room service

Haiku of Love and War

Elyse Braxton

I am out of touch
As I don't have Internet
At my beck and call

Way under budget
Although I didn't set one
I won't break the bank

I am overwhelmed
Not used to so much freedom
And retired life

Up at 8am
It's breakfast for everyone
I want to sleep in

We're out and about
I really want to relax
Recover my space

I understand now
Why convicts return to jail
Routine is their home

Please leave me alone
Feel like I'm being a bad guest
I just need my space

Thought I was immune
Because my leave was not home
Wrong, I still have stress

After a few days
Confessed freedom overload
They slowed down the pace

Playing Three Thirteen
A lovely little card game
For a rainy night

I have sticker shock
Everything's so expensive
Even if home grown

Indiana Jones
A movie for the big screen
What a thrill that was!

Town of Maleny
High in the Sunshine Coast
Honeymoon retreat

Shopping in Montville
Prices match the altitude
In the Blackall Range

Brisbane Museum
Featured all that's Australia
Focus on Queensland

Aborigines
Too fared discrimination
For having colour

Grandfather of mine
Aboriginal sailor
I'm in my gene pool

Haiku of Love and War

Seems colored people
No matter where in the world
Have faced challenges

Father give me strength
To submit my will to You
As I'll make a mess

Poor little old man
A widow for seven years
And very lonely

Asked for my email
He can have my Army one
It stops when I leave

I was just joking
When I said I had a "date"
He's too old for me

I saw a rainbow
Very faintly in the sky
Still it made my day

I was successful
Driving on the left-hand side
Hugged the center line

Most gorgeous sunsets
Grace the Pacific Ocean
And the mountain tops

The Shine Camp for girls
To help build their self-esteem
Before it's too late

We shared with the girls
How Jesus meets all our needs
Unlike those on Earth

Voice started to crack
When I talked about heartache
Caused by our father

Hearing the jazz show
I started to get lonely
So I took a walk

Sunday was quiet
As most of the stores were closed
So I window shopped

Humming songs of love
Took me back into your arms
Where I want to be

One week, I'll be gone
Then I'll be home in two months
Where did the time go?

Jamming on the drums
Uncle Howard kept the beat
Great to see him play

I'm a little down
But I know it's hormonal
Won't last forever

Sitting by myself
Yet surrounded by people
Heightened missing you

In her little world
The five-year old drew pictures
In her wedding dress

Her singing Mommy
Wore a dress that was too tight
And too revealing

Often there were times
I thought I could sing better
As I had more range

Here in Australia
They call it "America"
Not "United States"

Rain drops were falling
Believe this will help the drought
They say I'm good luck

Walking on the beach
The waves were crashing about
Hear the ocean's roar

It's all relative
Humidity I can't take
CAN handle the heat

Shopping the Gold Coast
Dropped a small fortune on opals
I have no regrets

Sure I've put on weight
I eat what's not in Kuwait
And sample new things

I'm not worried though
Soon diet and exercise
Back to my routine

A "casket" in Oz
A unique connotation
For a "treasure chest"

I'm a foreigner
Even though they speak English
The words aren't the same

At the morning tea
A woman liked my "accent"
But I don't have one

Things will get cooler
As we'll head towards Sydney
Hope we don't get rain

As I suspected
I packed more than I needed
That's the way it is

With the exchange rate
U.S. dollar is stronger
Still I shop wisely

The RSL clubs
Like the VFW
Without cigarettes

Playing the pokies
I made a profit last night
Not lucky today

Right at 6 o'clock
Oz version of "Taps" is played
At the RSL

Same pair of Levi's
Worn for almost two weeks now
Only pair of pants

Think my left ankle
Injury is why I walk
With some distinction

I've been successful
I haven't thought about work
It will still be there

Think about email
And if my mailbox is full
Upon my return

I can't remember
When do I go back to work?
Tuesday or Wednesday?

Trivia contest
At Katoomba RSL
We won the grand prize!!!

Shopped like a Sailor
Spent more than a thousand bucks
I have no remorse

Last part of my trip
Here in Sydney, Australia
Two more holi-days

Saw the Three Sisters
In the misty Blue Mountains
And cute waterfalls

Expensive Gold Coast
A true Surfer's Paradise
And lots of shopping

Our trivia prize
75 dollar gift
Voucher for meals

We splurged on dinner
Chinese food, drinks, and dessert
With change leftover

Pokies are her game
Aunt Robyn is "Lady Luck"
Won 54 bucks!!!

Sitting on a bench
Ferries sailing to and fro
Sky half blue, half grey

The cheapest thing here
A McDonald's ice cream cone
A mere 30 cents

Bought another ring
Rhodolite garnet, opals
The beauty haunts me

The sun's breaking through
But I still have my coat on
Over three layers

It's been two weeks now
Since I arrived "down under"
Where did the time go?

What shall I do here?
Just relax and see some sights
I like the down time

Head hurts a little
Hormones and dehydration
These things will happen

The sun feels so nice
It provides a touch of warmth
This fairly cool day

I've put on some weight
With all this nonstop eating
And trying new foods

No ibis birds here
Their fascinating black beaks
Scavenging for food

On the final stretch
85% finished
With my deployment

Keep the momentum
Slacking effects patient care
That is NEVER good

Liked watching rugby
Muscular men in short shorts
Yes, I'm a "leg man"

Australian football
People joke it's called Ping Pong
Like rugby better

What's a good sentence
For those caught misbehaving?
Cricket on TV

Back in our hotel
Heated games of Three Thirteen
Lots of trash talking

I learned a card trick!
I've never known one before
Can't wait to try it!

Said goodbye today
"Family" left for Brisbane
I stayed in Sydney

Sydney Harbor Bridge
Really just a bridge to me
I'm sorry Dundee

Sydney's like New York
More spread out and less crowded
They both have accents

I realized something
Haven't heard Spanish lately
I'm feeling homesick

Two months more or less
And I'll be in Maryland
What a year it's been

Adventure awaits
Ferry to Darling Harbor
Free jazz festival

The jazz singers sang
Sinatra, Martin, Darin
Of course I lip synced

As we sail along
I take in the ferry air
More like diesel fumes

Same street performer
Was spotted in three venues
Over two day's time

At the Opera House
Saw a "modern" performance
At least it was cheap

Watching the people
Dressed up every which a way
Walk the Sydney streets

At Taronga Zoo
Search for duckbill platypus
A mission failure

I love sea otters
Cute and forever playful
I'd watch them all day

Mighty leopard seal
Powerful in the water
Looks helpless on land

African meerkats
Remind me of prairie dogs
"Bathing" in heat lamps

I miss you so much
You went everywhere I went
As you're in my heart

At the jazz concert
I imagined us dancing
And the heat we'd make

Eyes locked and loaded
We are each other's target
We don't miss the mark

Dancing in your arms
Even if we're in a crowd
Feels like it's just us

I'm ever grateful
To have swum in my gene pool
There's a sense of pride

Catching my eye
Aboriginal artwork
Sense of belonging

Pride in heritage
My Aboriginal roots
No matter how small

Now I'm coming home
Goodbye to shoes and earrings
Hello uniform

Reality break
I can't believe it's over
A great holiday

I'll be home Monday
Can't wait to swim and salsa
Burn some calories

Dutiful servant
The little old man met me
Right at baggage claim

Felt obligated
To have tea and make small talk
As he is lonely

I love my new ring
The rainbow of the opals
A fire within

I have no regrets
For extending six months
The trip was worth it

Now in Singapore
Two more flights and I'll be home
Beloved desert

Almost three weeks now
That I haven't worn my boots
That'll change quickly

Ankles are swollen
Due to 16 flight hours
Plus lack of movement

Last leg of travel
Reality awaits me
It's been a good trip

Last taste of freedom
Cold Stone Creamery ice cream
Breakfast of heroes

Scent of cigarettes
Smoke wafts through the terminal
Assault to my nose

Last leg of Kuwait marathon

Compassion fatigue
Caregivers need caring too
Though hard to admit

When you are deployed
It's said you have blinders on
I reckon it's true

I have to admit
I'm not lonely when deployed
That may not be good

What I mean by that
We are all in the same boat
Even playing field

That's not fully true
We're all lonely together
Than just lonely me

Desire for love
That elusive emotion
I hope it finds me

These are all I have
Deepest longings of my heart
As I am single

With time on my hands
My mind wanders all over
Mostly about love

Time spent with the Lord
I give Him my frustrations
What am I to do?

Having a hard time
Giving my will up to God
Want to do His will

I search the Bible
Guidance and direction sought
From God's holy Word

A blast from the past
A chaplain assistant friend
From five years ago

I like attention
From those who don't shave their legs
And have deep voices

Not looking for love
Would like male companionship
'Cause they're not women

I dream of romance
As most girls do, gay or straight
We're wired that way

How do I manage?
I tend to read love stories
By fiction writers

Haiku of Love and War

A colleague asked me
What do I do after work?
Didn't really know

I thought about it
I told her about haiku
Dancing and woodshop

I keep to myself
As the new kid in the bay
But I'm still friendly

Haiku and sleeping
Just two ways to pass the time
Need to exercise

Once I'm back stateside
I will face reality
I hope it looks good

One day at a time
It's the only way to live
Yeah, tell my mind that!

What would it be like?
If I were an Admiral
I'd still just be me

No matter how high
I climb the Officer ranks
I will seek to serve

Lord, reveal to me
What I am supposed to do
I'm anxious to know

I'm fully aware
God's timing is successful
Whereas mine isn't

Hurry up and wait
Military invention
Now it's perfected

I'm getting sleepy
It's not even 9pm
There's nothing to do

Think I'll go to bed
But some Bible verses first
Simulcast scriptures

Amazing longing
I'm feeling depressed right now
I miss you so much

I've been down all day
As we are separated
Tugging at my heart

All I do is sleep
Don't feel like socializing
As in no salsa

I feel the lyrics
"So lost in love without you"
I'm truly empty

Haiku of Love and War

How will I survive?
Once I have demobilized
It won't be easy

Hey, let's runaway
Romeo and Juliet
But no suicide

I just go to bed
When my workday is over
Don't want to go out

Miss your attention
I'll take it from anywhere
Temporary thought

I stay in my room
Just want to be by myself
Sadness runs its course

Temporary fix
Two troops from my past
Happy distractions

Time to stay grounded
With Jesus, Lord and Savior
Band-Aid® for my heart

Nice thing about work
The busyness masks the pain
But then I go home

Feeling mighty blue
Palpable separation
Minor depression

I will seize the day
Snap out of this funk I'm in
Yes, this too shall pass

Feeling MUCH better
Couldn't spend another day
Feeling that lousy

Back in bed again
Finished watching the movie
Now what's there to do?

Deployment's not real
It's where time is forgotten
The world's not on hold

We're all better now
Just needed to blow off steam
Back to the loving

Mutual tears shed
About this amazing love
That's only begun

Like a prisoner
You're denied your basic rights:
Love and affection

Whenever there's growth
Pain is likely to proceed
It's simple as that

Haiku of Love and War

Elyse Braxton

We give and receive
The love God supplies daily
As fast as we can

Into three small words
We summarize the Bible
It says, "God is love"

I can't imagine
Being separated from
God's absolute love

Fighting back her tears
They had to say their goodbyes
She ran back to him

The two young lovers
United in purity
Divided by work

In the loading zone
Last minute hugs and kisses
Until he returns

Interchangeable
The meanings of God and love
They're one in the same

When we're together
We could just 'be' and have fun
Because of God's love

Still very content
I knew it wouldn't last long
That bump in the road

As I've said before
When I want your attention
I tend to pick fights

The joy of dancing
I'm following the leader
Perfect harmony

Couldn't stop smiling
It's been so long since I've danced
I still had my moves!

My buddy Gary
Claimed me as his own tonight
We're good dance partners

A pesky side stitch
Prevented my enjoyment
Of the merengue

Counting down the days
The staff is getting anxious
For their departure

I have mixed feelings
I've "nursed" longer in Kuwait
Than I have at home

Mom's been so helpful
In getting my home ready
For my first renter

How can I repay
My Mom for all she has done?
I'd say she's priceless

I don't understand
Why they hate being deployed
I just dealt with it

If not for salsa
This deployment would be hard
It's the great escape

It's nice to be missed
By my junior troops up north
I made an impact

Despite the mistakes
Which are few and far between
I still love my job

It just gets me though
There's little personal praise
But they point fingers

May God provide you
The desires of your heart
Because He loves you

Dancing's so much fun
Unofficial instructor
I teach in the hall

Waiting patiently
So that we can dance salsa
Show me what you got!

Off to woodshop
Want to make tea light holders
For me and my friends

A simple design
Four-inch hearts made from walnut
With my heart and hands

Thinking out my plan
I will stain them with bee's wax
To highlight the grain

Sunday's their big day
Our replacements will deploy
Three weeks they'll be here

The end's coming near
I'm starting to realize
The length of my tour

Really should be proud
I've done a year in Kuwait
Most have done 6 months

Was happy to learn
We will land in Baltimore
And not Atlanta

Now there is a chance
That I can see my parents
Upon our return

Thought it was a date
When he invited me out
Mistaken meaning

Seems after salsa
They have an after party
Over in Zone 6 six

Expressed my concerns
About fraternization
Now we understand

Like Cinderella
Some girls tried on the black heals
They only fit me

I haven't worn heals
In well over a year now
I'm EVEN taller!

I feel so welcome
Though I'm really a stranger
In the Latin world

Of all the things here
I will miss Latin dancing
The most in Kuwait

My stomach's nervous
Because it's almost over
This is what I know

Notification
Have to see the DNS
Now, no appetite

Know what's terrible?
I always assume the worst
When they ask for me

What is it about?
Why does she want to see me?
This is killing me!

Ever paranoid
Of getting into trouble
Help my unbelief

The sheer agony
Soles of my feet are sweaty
Can I see her now?

Great for my figure
My stomach is all in knots
I do something wrong?

Sack cloth and ashes
It's a way to show the world
That I'm suffering

Wasn't in trouble
Admiral requested me
For teleconference

When I'm a leader
I'll start my sentences with
"You're not in trouble"

Like a great gymnast
I "nailed" my portion of the
Video conf'rence

Admiral B-K
Of all the people she met
I got the sole hug

Pizza and near beer
The Admiral wore flip flops
A true Jersey girl

After our dinner
Admiral wanted to chat
She came after me!

Nose not really brown
We're Villanova nurses
She liked my story

I'm truly humbled
That I know "important" folks
Who'd more than help me

At the Corpsman Ball
I won an iPod shuffle
A true gift from God

Equally super
A girlfriend won a day off
Spent it with her love

Counting down the weeks
Almost time to redeploy
Extremely anxious

Jail for good people
This is my reality
Yes, it's abnormal

Time to readjust
I need to be deprogrammed
Acclimate to States

Alienation
I have felt it all along
Since I extended

They have their networks
I feel like an outsider
But we're still a team

He knew where I stood
I feel like a heartbreaker
I just can't "go there"

I can do group things
Not solo with enlisted
It's "against the law"

The one nurse I know
Wears her grandmother's diamond
To ward off the men

False environment
Men and women are caged in
We're free but locked in

I lift up my hands
High to Your home in Heaven
Father, hear my prayer

Father, You heard me
Words of thanksgiving and praise
You always come through

First time to hitchhike
But I'm on a secure base
I know Mom would laugh

Laughed with my driver
Mom would be so proud of me
I was resourceful

Arriving in style
In an air-conditioned car
I thanked my driver

The Fourth of July
Was like any other day
Here on deployment

Well, I take that back
Red, white and blue was abound
But no fireworks

Atlanta Peachtree
10 Kilometer Road Race
The Kuwait Time Group

I met all my goals
I ran the entire course
And got the T-shirt

Patriotic lei
Worn over my DCU's
Special occasion

Was SO excited
I've never run a 10k
Up for the challenge

It was a slow pace
But I turn on the burners
When the end's in sight

One more "to do" done
A movie night with MARCENT
With friends old and new

Days are winding down
Thinking about my parents
Gets me teary-eyed

I haven't seen them
Since I left them in July
And soon, face to face

Mom's been SO helpful
To me since I've been deployed
HER, Navy service

Not enough money
In the world to pay her back
For all she has done

Dad has been helping
In his special kind of way
It touches Mom's heart

I'll miss "Mi Gente"
That's Spanish for "My people"
Friends on the dance floor

Had a banned substance
It is called "Gasolina"
Some kind of rum drink

A birthday dinner
Shared with a friend from boot camp
Old friends are the best!

A trip into town
The last for our detachment
Glad I got to go

I bought perfumed oil
Alcohol's banned in Kuwait
Scented souvenir

Counting down the days
As we'll be leaving Kuwait
Almost a whole year

Already one year
Since I left for deployment
Miss parents and friends

Working like a fiend
In the super-hot woodshop
They've been so helpful

Always creative
Dif'rent woods and finishes
For items I'll use

Less sentimental
How I'm currently feeling
It is sure to change

The elliptical:
Operation Khakis Fit
My secret weapon

Keep the momentum
The patients depend on us
We can't slack off now

Strawberry cigar
To smoke with my MARCENT friends
I belong with them

Counting my blessings
For all the people I know
And their influence

Softball with MARCENT
The Colonel called me to bat
I hit a single!!!

Burger Burn goodbye
I networked with the Colonel
It was nice bonding

Haiku of Love and War

Elyse Braxton

It is not normal
To deploy for a whole year
Toll on the body

One day at a time
Soon we'll be reunited
With our families

I made a flag box
With help from my woodshop friends
Will hand carry home

Saluting sharply
The flag to honor my Mom
Flown on her birthday

Mom's a true hero
Her support of OIF
And me was awesome

Talking about Mom
Often brings tears to my ears
She has done SO much!

I am not normal
THIS is my reality
I'm scared to go home

Savor the moments
Make "checks" in my "to do list"
As I leave Kuwait

Forming some closure
A hug from a housekeeper
Saying my goodbyes

Movies with my friends
Sharing meals in the DFAC
Treasuring the time

Packing up my stuff
Returning battle rattle
Mailing things back home

Woodshop family
Workers and helpers alike
Will truly miss them

Friday night salsa
Three more dances left for me
Then I have to go

Sergeant Garcia
A consistent friendly face
I'll really miss him

I was scared to leave
I'm not feeling that way now
Ready to go home

Packing up my things
As I scavenge for boxes
To mail my stuff home

Looking for handouts
The TCNs have little
We gave shoes and clothes

Haiku of Love and War

Elyse Braxton

Feeling overwhelmed
Many people under foot
While I do my job

Holding back the tears
I'm incredibly stressed out
Yet I must press on

A colleague told me
That (we) nurses are givers
Who are still in need

Battle rattle's gone
We returned that on Sunday
Now there's time to kill

Watching a movie
With one of my Major friends
Dinner afterwards

Saying my goodbyes
I still have photos to take
Memories of Kuwait

I witnessed a birth
Heriberto's born again
On 20 July

Couldn't stop crying
Tears - a symbol of cleansing
He is a new man

A nice faith based chat
Over dinner and Starbuck's
He's feeling peaceful

You said you were proud
As I deployed for a year
I finished the race

I am so thankful
No Red Cross messages, no
Emergency leave

It's affecting me
I'm coming to realize
My year's deployment

Slowly giving in
The fact that I'm going home
Okay, I'm ready

We're twiddling our thumbs
For the most part, we are done
Just waiting to leave

Last minute errands
I have more shopping to do
Impulse buys, for sure

I'm feeling lonely
No significant other
Home for my return

They all have someone
Spouses and children waiting
I feel out of place

Haiku of Love and War

I keep to myself
With bottled up misery
Semi-denial

Don't feel important
Seeking public approval
It's God's that matters

Feeling like a freak
So outgoing but single
Hard to believe

Is there any one
Who will take a chance on me?
Someone to love me?

There's always Jesus
He won't leave or forsake me

He is all I need
Halt my selfishness
I need to count my blessings
I have so many

I want to be held
To be told I'm beautiful
And that I am loved

As I get older
It seems my chances for love
Continue to shrink

My job and schooling
Will take up most of my time
Then I go to sleep

I keep my chin up
When there's talk about loved ones
It's just not my time

satan is tricky
he knows every weakness
pushes those buttons

Feel like a bridesmaid
In that I never get picked
An accessory

Great joy from dancing
With people who make me smile
As they touch my heart

Please come after me
I'm tired of pursuing
Folks for attention

At the post office
Rifling through my underwear
And everything else

We had our briefing
No real focus on singles
Kinda bummed me out

Dancing with MARCENT
Salsa on the patio
They're both quick studies

Our farewell dinner
The CO got teary eyed
Leader and lady

Deployment bracelet
Created by a Corpsman
A sweet young lady

Last night for salsa
A photo with my buddy
And dance with a "pro"

One soldier dancer
With the very sweaty hands
And his flashy moves

Prefer the Latinos
They excel on the dance floor
It is their birthright

I must remember
That I'm an American
Learning MY dance steps

Taking some photos
Capturing the memories
Of my boots on sand

Seems we're 3%
Of Sailors who are IA's
Truly a rare breed

The chaplain told us
We should expect depression
As we readjust

Wish there was someone
Waiting for me to come home
Alas it's just me

Song with DFA
Concert in the laundry room
Flack and Hathaway

Emotional tank
It feels like it's on empty
Or it's getting there

Cleaning up my room
Picking up and throwing out
We leave on Friday

Last night in Kuwait

Fellow salsero
Alone in an ER bed
I stayed by her side

My friend was in pain
She didn't need loneliness
As a companion

Four hours later
We rode the bus to her zone
Jesus would do this

Miscarriage or not
She will find out on Monday
My friend is peaceful

The longer I nurse
I learn of man's frailty
How could I throw stones?

Re-deploying/ Back Home

The final lockdown
Here we are at Ali Al Salem
Before we go home

Working party formed
As we unload our seabags
Please pass the Motrin®

Next onto customs
Through the metal detectors
Onto the worst part

First unpack your bags
Customs goes through ev'rything
Then bags are repacked

The crying has stopped
Least till I see my parents
Then bawl my eyes out

Had my last goodbyes
Meals with important people
All get hugs, some tears

I did it my way
I had closure on my terms
I have no regrets

Still get teary eyed
Thinking about my mother
And our reunion

The cloud has lifted
I can't turn back, I'm at peace
And I'm going home

How WILL I react?
Once I return from Kuwait
Will I get depressed?

Still feel out of place
Never felt like I fit in
Like I'm a step-child

Muster and roll call
Our last name or last four
The military

So many boxes
To unpack when I get home
A year's worth of stuff

The working party
All the junior enlisted
Officers, exempt

Can't wait to see them
Last seen in July, last year
Before I deployed

How will I have changed?
I know I have more grey hair
Parents getting old

I kept my boots on
Even though I'm sure my feet
Have swollen in flight

Leipzig Germany
We could buy ourselves a "toast"
I had some Asti

Army's flying too
But they're not allowed to drink
We won't drink on plane

Sitting with Wendy
A strong nurse of faith my age
We're in business class

God's favor again
Divine seating provided
Little more leg room

It's like a cloud broke
The stressors dissipated
Least they have for now

Got in the last call
Before we boarded the bus
In touch with my love

Morning wakeup call
I'm sure a bleeding fortune
But SO well worth it

That AT&T
Eats phone card minutes faster
Than eating contests

Tears come to your eyes
As you share your beaming pride
In what I have done

Hasn't sunk in yet
The fact that I did one year
A good career move?

The soldiers with us
Did 15 months in Iraq
Did they lose some troops?

So far no soreness
Dealing with all the luggage
Here's hoping never

I saw stars last night
And clouds were in the sky, TWICE!
Rare gifts of beauty

Seems troops from up north
Think Kuwait is very hot
This was all I knew

Heat versus combat
I'll take the heat any day
Can live without fear

How will I have changed?
Now that I'm redeploying
Only time will tell

Catching free movies
National Anthem is played
Before every film

Six boxes of stuff
Hold things I've had here with me
Will bring less next time

Asked about my year
The first Det was easier
Felt like I belonged

I could do a year
If we deploy as one group
Not two detachments

This won't be my last
Time I'll receive combat pay
My career is young

Military day
Is not 24 hours
More like 36

Hurry up and wait
Is the theme of a lifetime
For the Armed Forces

Will they applaud us
When we first go through customs?
What's awaiting us?

Back in the United States

Airport reunion
Mom was the first one I saw
I took her picture

The biggest surprise?
Seeing Evan and Richard
Then my tears started

Knowing me that well
Mom had a pack of tissues
For just that reason

Evan called Stan
For a welcome home by phone
The mission: complete

Evan and Richard
Assisted the USO
To make goodie bags

Missing the free food
Mostly desserts and veggies
Didn't have to cook

Mom brought me roses
Returning warrior gift
For our reunion

In their summer whites
We were greeted with handshakes
Welcomes and thank yous

Lined up in a row
Stood the welcome committee
What an awesome sight

Down the handshake line
One man embraced me tightly
Longer than normal

Was a little weird
But it wasn't a "bad touch"
He said he could cry

"You from Bethesda?"
"Yes." "Good, then report Monday."
What a welcome home!

I'm very happy
I didn't bawl my eyes out
As I thought I would

A warm welcome home
And the most perfect weather
Truly planned by God

Over to Fort Meade
To hit the commissary
As my fridge was bare

In my DCU's
I thought more people would know
I'd come home from war

21 July
Last time I slept in my bed
Mattress I longed for

My first deployment
Three hundred eighty-four days
I've come a long way

Know what I'm missing?
Housekeepers and free food
And salsa, of course

Free bottled water
Is now ancient history
Back to drinking tap

No more dorm bathroom
A single toilet and sink
Ditch the shower shoes

Got my car started
Evan and I went for a drive
I even drove fast!

It's been a long while
Since I've driven a stick shift
Didn't stall it once

Elyse Braxton — Haiku of Love and War

The comforts of home
I can do what I want to
Freedom is tasty

Tall soy chai latte
They don't have them in Kuwait
Had my first last night

Still light at 7
It would be dark in Kuwait
And in the 90's

Going through the mail
What to keep and what to toss
What goes to shredder

Just as I figured
Mom brought a cooler of food
For the five of us

I am not picky
As I will eat airplane food
Whatever they have

Tried on my khakis
Yes, they were a little snug
But that's soon to change

No more free desserts
Goodbye pie, cake, and ice cream
Too cheap to buy them

Boo hoo salad bar
I will miss all the veggies
No prep time for me

Weigh 129
I am sure some is muscle
Some of it is not

Goodbye my young men
Evan and Richard are off
Mom and Dad stay on

Getting them settled
Mom and Dad stayed overnight
Church in the morning

After services
We drove to the hospital
To run some errands

Saw some folks I knew
Hadn't really hit me yet
Still in shock, I guess

All By Myself

Parents left Sunday
It hit me, I was alone
Full of new sadness

All alone, again
I was denied solitude
For over a year

Elyse Braxton — Haiku of Love and War

Sat there paralyzed
Left to my own devices
With no one around

Went to bed early
I had nothing to "live" for
Mission: completed

Up with the roosters
Back into my DCU's
My return to work

Monday was check-in
I felt like an outsider
NOT a good feeling

Holding back the tears
Loneliness was palpable
I didn't belong

With papers in hand
The wild goose chase had begun
To get signatures

Computer passwords
Travel claims and medical
Got to get it done

Make the appointments
Hurry up and wait again
Some things never change

In our DCU's
We're set apart from the rest
Spoils for the victor?

They said I "looked great"
I'd like to know what they see
Uniform, perhaps?

Felt isolated
They talked of a barbeque
No invite for me

I had forewarning
The second Det would be rough
No prescribed bonding

Ever the step-child
I did what I did to cope
As I had six months

My Department Head
Granted me two more weeks leave
Because of my year

My first reaction
Was that two weeks was too much
I would go crazy

In my apartment
Boxes are my companions
Yet I'm still lonely

Wallowing around
I deal with my loneliness
And I ride their waves

I still have jetlag
I'm seven hours ahead
Up WAY too early

Gone for a whole year
I can't run straight back to work
Must recuperate

I need to stay home
Get used to being Stateside
Fourteen days of leave

Mom kept calling me
But my cell phone was turned off
She was worrying

She called Jean and Pam
To see if they heard from me
Feeling desperate

"Mom, my phone was off"
Concerned about my safety
Upon my return

She read the brochures
From Fleet Family Support
About depression

"I'll call once a day
To let you know I'm all right"
The least I can do

Calls to long lost friends
We'll meet here and in New York
Can't wait to see them

Radhika's coming
To DC for a meeting
We'll meet for dinner

Riding two Metros
And a bus to get to her
My dinner was free

"You're staying over
I want to make sure you're safe"
How could I fight her?

What will I sleep in?
I made a blanket toga
Perfect pajamas

Big girl sleepover
We talked about war and love
We look like sisters

Spontaneously
I crashed their breakfast meeting
Then hugged her goodbye

Exploring outside
Beauty of the Potomac
And the hotel grounds

With camera in hand
Was a glorified tourist
In my own country

Beauty of flowers
You can't take them for granted
A feast for my eyes

Dinner at Pam's house
My lonely feelings came back
Will I get married?

Watching Olympics
Phelps got the gold in the Fly
This was his seventh

Internal struggle
I seek to be a leader
Yet I'm low in rank

Most of my age peers
Manage departments or troops
I want to be BIG!

Career frustration
What IS it I want to do?!
I want to be "boss"

Some doors are closed though
Because of my "advanced age"
No use fighting it

Slightly defeated
I'll find what's out there for me
I will stay Navy

Late nights of research
Surfing on the Internet
Brain locked and loaded

Wise counsel again
Don't have set goals right now
Thus personal stress

Evan was in town
We grabbed Chipotle for lunch
Watched a DVD

Hometown Homecoming

Driving to Philly
In the rush hour traffic
Like riding a bike

Yearly Barbeque
By Special Athlete sponsors
I wouldn't miss it

Familiar faces
Got lots of hugs and kisses
Felt good to be home

Once at Mom and Dad's
I got settled in my room
Repeat hug from Dad

Errands with Colleen
Phillies game with cousin Jean
Shopped at the mall

Talking on my cell
Under a shady birch tree
Watching kids at play

In a state of thanks
I touch trees and look at bugs
Funny what you miss

When was the last time
You stopped to smell the flowers?
Taken for granted

I got to salsa
Received a hero's welcome
I fought back the tears

Dancing was awesome
I really followed their lead
Had lots of practice

I like a leader
As I'll follow his dance steps
No hesitation

At my old Squadron
I hug my fellow shipmates
Old and new faces

Talking to Senior
I did what I said I'd do
He said I was "Rare"

Back in my khakis
I didn't feel out of place
In the hospital

By the grace of God
I met with the detailer
For next assignment

Afternoon briefings
For the Nurse Corps Officers
Glad I had the time

Getting clarity
Not sure about FNP
NOT time for grad school

My first deployment
Three hundred eighty-four days
No need for tattoo

I went on a date
I am SO not used to this
It's been a long time

What's he want from me?
What is he thinking about?
I don't like dating

I could call him up
He did give me his number
Way to kill some time

What if I call him?
Will I appear desperate?
I am so confused

Just wanna be friends
My modus operandi
For self-protection

Wish I had someone
So I wouldn't be "out there"
God, what IS your plan?

I want what I want
I enjoy male attention
And have my freedom

I'm feeling lonely
Wish I was back in Kuwait
There'd be stuff to do

Some days are harder
I just want to see Jesus
Leave this place called Earth

Not suicidal
But I cannot wait to die
Go home to Heaven

It's Saturday night
I'm surfing the Internet
Such a party girl

The leaves are falling
Hear the crunching underfoot
I don't have to rake

Time to walk the dog
People and their furry friends
Checking out nature

Career direction
Time to achieve my set goals
One step at a time

Okinawa-bound
Time to serve with my Marines
Scared but excited

The old me is home
I'm back on the career path
I have direction

A hurricane hit
Right here in my apartment
It came from Kuwait

A change of command
For my Vice Admiral friend
Such a special day

At ceremony
Memento for Ensign Boot
Coin from CNO

He will thank his wife
I will get emotional
As I always do

Will I have someone
Of significance to thank
When I retire?

Haiku of Love and War

Braxton reunion
The 5 of us together
A long time coming

Oldies and goodies
Elton John, Harry Chapin
CD's are playing

Folks playing scrabble
Or electronic device
We're all together

Futon for parents
My brothers slept in my bed
I slept on the floor

Standing in the heat
As we're waiting to be cleared
Into the White House

Folks making small talk
Presidential volunteers
And their families

In Service Dress Whites
I render salutes smartly
To military

The President spoke
Michael W. Smith sang
We toured the White House

Riding the subway
On the way to dinner
We see a cousin

She's asked to join us
Ethiopian cuisine
And Dad paid the bill

As soon as they came
My family left as quickly
And my house was clean

Little souvenir
My combat zone currency
Paper coins called "Pogs"

Epilogue

I had my first exposure to the Japanese poetry form of haiku in elementary school. I'm almost positive I viewed this 3 lined 5-7-5 syllable written art form with the same disdain I had for most vegetables. They were required, I complied, but they were not liked. As I matured and came to tolerate most vegetables, the memory of haiku resurfaced one day while reading poetry. I loved being able to paint word pictures of emotions and observations with 17 syllables. I was drawn to the rhythm as evidenced by drumming my fingers to count the syllables as words popped into my head.

I was called to deploy to Kuwait my first year in the Navy Nurse Corps. With lots of time on my hands I took to writing haiku to keep my mind entertained. Over the course of a year plus, I wrote over 3,000 haiku. (Yes, I like and liked to keep my mind amused.) I captured personal experiences and observations. I especially enjoyed writing vicarious haiku as it stretched my mind to imagine what it was like to be someone else and their experiences.

As I organized the haiku, I found it interesting that after all this time some things remained crystal clear yet other memories (stress and stressors) faded away. I'm glad on both accounts. I also feel scared yet brave because I exposed vulnerabilities and insecurities from that time in my life. I am comforted knowing I am not alone as other women have experienced the same emotions and thoughts, whether in uniform or not. Same heart, different bodies. I am pleased I have grown so much spiritually, personally, and professionally in the years following my deployment. I love growing older because of the added security and surety of self. God's not done with me, or any of us, yet. There's still more haiku to write.
Stay tuned.

Glossary

AJ – Camp Arijan, Kuwait

Ali Al Salem – air base in Kuwait

ARCENT- U.S. Army Central

ATV – All-terrain vehicle

Battle buddy – partner and/or friend to ensure mutual safety

Battle rattle – full combat gear

Bethesda – National Naval Medical Center, Bethesda, MD, now Walter Reed National Military Medical Center

Body armor – bullet resistant vest that can be modified with throat, shoulder, and groin protection.

Boot Ensign – junior most Ensign within a Naval command

Butter Bar – nickname for an Ensign or 2nd Lieutenant as signified by their gold bar rank collar device. Lowest officer rank.

Cadets – nickname for U.S. Military Academy students

C-17 – military cargo and transport aircraft

Camelbak®- hydration source

Civies – civilian (non-military) clothing

CNO – Chief of Naval Operations. Four-star admiral and senior most naval officer in the Department of the Navy

CO – Commanding Officer, also known as Skipper

Commissary – military "supermarket"

Concertina wire – razor or barbed wire formed in large coils to serve as military boundaries and obstacles.

Cover – hat

Corpsman/men – enlisted medical specialist/s in the United States Navy

Cougar – an older woman who pursues younger men

DCU – U.S. Armed Forces Desert Camouflage Uniform

Det – Detachment

DFA – Director for Administration

DFAC – Dining Facility also known as mess or chow hall. Navy/Coast Guard equivalent is "galley"

Divo – Division Officer

DNS – Director for Nursing Services

DSN – Defense Switched Network. Worldwide telephone system for the U.S. Department of Defense

FNP – Family Nurse Practitioner

Four-star – unspoken nickname of a full admiral or general as signified by their four star rank collar device. Highest officer rank

4th ID – U.S. Army Fourth Infantry Division based in Fort Carson, Colorado

Fraternization - an unduly familiar personal relationship between an officer and an enlisted that does not respect the difference in rank or grade

Groundhog Day – based off the movie, of the same name, to describe deployment as every day is the same regardless of how one tries to change it

Guidon – military flag to signify unit designation

Helo – helicopter

IA – Individual Augmentee. A military member assigned to a unit for a temporary duty assignment

J.G. – nickname for Navy/Coast Guard rank of Lieutenant Junior Grade. Signified by a silver bar rank collar device.

Kevlar – helmet made with 19 layers of ballistic resin of the same name

Khakis – Service Khaki uniform worn by Navy Chief Petty Officers and Officers

Leave - vacation

L.T. – nickname for a Lieutenant Junior Grade (LTJG) or Lieutenant (LT)

Litter – folding metal gurney for transporting patients in military ambulances and aircraft.

M16 – U.S. military rifle

MARCENT – Marine Corps Forces Central Command

Master Chief – nickname for Navy/Coast Guard rank for Master Chief Petty Officer

MOPP gear – Mission Oriented Protective Posture used to protect U.S. military from chemical, biological, radiological, and nuclear strikes

MP – Military police

MRE – Meal Ready to Eat (prepackaged, precooked meals for U.S. troops)

Mustang – an Officer who was promoted up through the enlisted ranks, also known as "prior service."

PT/gear – physical training/gear

Pogs – paper coins, that are not legal tender in the United States, used in place of metal coins by Army Air Force Exchange Services to reduce weight of shipment of currency to combat zones

Pokies – Australian slot machines

Rating – Navy enlisted occupational specialty

Red Badge – color of badge issued to members holding Secret Clearance with the Department of Defense, Department of Homeland Security, and Central Intelligence Agency (CIA)

Red Cross Message – a service provided by the American Red Cross to deliver emergency messages, such as death or serious illness, to Armed Forces service members anywhere in the world. This information is used by the service member and their commanding officer when determining the need to take emergency leave

R&R – Rest and recuperation/relaxation

RSL – Returned and Services League of Australia for men and women who served in Australian Defense Force

Sacred Twenty – the first female nurses to serve in the newly created Navy Nurse Corps

Summer Whites – Summer uniform of the day worn for office work, business ashore, etc.

TCN – Third-Country National – contracted employee whose nationality is different from the country in which s/he is hired to work in

Seabag – duffel bag

SEA hut – Southeast Asia huts original built for use in Vietnam for U.S. troops' berthing

Senior – nickname for Navy/Coast Guard enlisted rank of Senior Chief Petty Officer

Service Dress Whites – seasonal uniform worn by Navy Chief Petty Officers and Officers for official events that do not require full or formal attire. Civilian equivalent of a business suit.

Shukran - "Thank you/I thank you a lot" in Arabic

Skipper – also known as CO

Taps – bugle call played at dusk, during military funerals, and flag ceremonies by the U.S. Armed Forces

Ugly Betty – nickname from my cousin because military women are often unrecognizable out of uniform considering the grooming standards we're to adhere to.

USO – United Service Organizations. Nonprofit organization that provides programs, live entertainment, etc. to U.S. Armed Forces members and their families worldwide

Wardroom – a cabin in which officers on a naval vessel gather to dine and recreate. The term also applies to those eligible to occupy the wardroom. Primarily a Navy tradition, a wardroom is also applicable to officers of the sea services (Marine Corps and Coast Guard)

VFW – Veterans of Foreign Wars of the U.S.

About the Author

Socially awkward
Must be kept on a long leash
Student of the world

Bold woman of faith
Calculated risk taker
Quirky, delightful

Volunteer spirit
Card carrying introvert
Overthink too much

Believer in dreams
Self-professed networking fool
Loving team player

Goal oriented
Loyal Philadelphian
Multifaceted

Adventure seeker
Adult impersonator
First born, two brothers

Elyse Braxton was deployed to Kuwait as an Individual Augmentee, with the United States Navy, in support of Operation Iraqi Freedom from July 2007 to August 2008. She served as a Staff Nurse at the United States Military Hospital Kuwait Expeditionary Medical Facility at Camp Arifjan and at the Troop Medical Center at Camp Buehring.

Ms. Braxton enlisted in the United States Navy Reserve in April 2003, in an Aviation rating, and graduated as the Distinguished Graduate from boot camp in October 2003. It was, in December 2003, during her second volunteer vacation to serve at, the United States Army, Landstuhl Regional Medical Center, in Germany, that she was divinely inspired to become a nurse. She was commissioned as an Ensign in the United States Navy Nurse Corps upon her graduation from Villanova University's College of Nursing in July 2006.

It is the author's wish to share her thoughts, feelings, dreams, observations, and prayers captured from the full circle perspective of a woman deploying for the first time.

I like the order
Of the Japanese haiku
Short and to the point

'Tis ever constant
The rhythm of a haiku
Like a beating heart

My book of haiku
A journal through poetry
Memories forever

Elyse Braxton	Haiku of Love and War